★ ★ ★ ★ ★

JAMES, HAPPY UNCLE

My nephew doesn't love reading and it's hard to find anything to keep his attention. He read two stories the first night and anytime I see him he has a new fact or bit of a story he wants to tell me about.

★ ★ ★ ★ ★

CLEONA, PROUD MUM OF GIRLS

My daughter already loves sports and even though it's improving, most of the sports stars she sees are men. I bought this for her because of the female role models. She couldn't hear enough about Katie Taylor and Yusra Mardini and the others, and has already taken some of the life lessons on board.

★ ★ ★ ★ ★

ADDISON, 10

My dad got me this. I really enjoyed all the stories. The pictures were awesome too. We talked a lot about the stories and the different sports. I told my friends about it too.

★ ★ ★ ★ ★

BARBARA, MIDDLE SCHOOL TEACHER

I bought this for my ELA class because of the diverse athletes and uplifting stories. And it's been on continuous rotation since. One of our sixth graders loved it and showed his classmates. Now they all want their turn. Might have to get another one.

★ ★ ★ ★ ★

ROBERTO, BASEBALL COACH

This book blows open the myth that the top athletes are just 'talented' and really shows the hard work and determination that's needed. The kids I coach were getting discouraged after a winless season thinking that the other teams were 'just better' than them. I recommended this book to a few of the parents and the feedback has been amazing. Some of the kids can't wait to get back to practice for next season and tell me about all th extra bits they are doing at home because of what they read in the book. Better than any speech I could give them!

★ ★ ★ ★ ★

TIM, DAD TO ROWDY BOYS

I have two boys, 8 & 12. They've been working through this together with my oldest reading alot of the stories to his little brother. It's fun to see them getting excited about sports, but also just to see them enjoying reading and learning new words together is heartwarming. I've also enjoyed the chatting to them about some of the older athletes like Bill Russell, brings back some nice memories.

INSPIRING SPORTS STORIES FOR CURIOUS KIDS

Delve into the tales of 14 remarkable athletes as they
defy the odds to make their dreams come true.

AIDAN HOGAN

IT'S HARD TO BEAT A PERSON WHO NEVER GIVES UP.

BABE RUTH

IN THIS B

WHAT'S S GREAT ABO SPORTS ANYWAY?

We all know that sport is awesome, right? But have you ever stopped to think why we love it so much? What is it that makes us want to dive in a muddy field to catch a ball or to put posters of football players on our bedroom walls?

Everyone loves sport for different reasons.

Maybe you play sports yourself or maybe you have a nice memory of kicking a ball around with your mom or dad, or watching an exciting game on TV?

All of these experiences make you feel a different way. Sport can make us happy, sad, excited, frustrated, anxious, joyful. So many emotions! People are drawn towards emotions. Take this for example; have you ever tried to remember a movie you saw a couple of years ago - you can't remember the details like the names of the characters, but you can remember exactly how it made you feel? That's because we remember emotions more than facts and figures. And this is where sport comes into its own.

All great sporting achievements tell a story that rides the wave of emotions. Stories of perseverance, friendship, victory, or loss can take hold of us and carry us on an exciting journey.

Athletes become heroes (villains too sometimes), rival teams face off in games that almost feel like life or death. And sometimes amazing things happen - a girl grows up in a country where boxing isn't allowed but goes on to become the world champion. Or a high-school science teacher becomes a pitcher in major league baseball!

Would you like to hear a few of these stories?

Then follow me through the pages of this book. You will hear about athletes who should never have succeeded, because they were too small, too tall or a different color. Or because they were poor or ill. But their determination & love of sport drove them on.

Ready? Then turn the page and let's get started.

TONY HAWK

It was the 1999 X-Games. Hawk was on the half-pipe. He had just done his best trick, a spectacular 720. He was the clear winner but still had ten minutes left in his run. Now what? In his mind there was only one place left to go.

Over the previous ten years, Hawk had been working on the '900', a trick where he launches himself as high as possible and does two-and-a-half mid-air spins before landing. This trick had never been done before. The two spins it required meant that Hawk would lose sight of his landing spot twice. No other move had this and it's why it was so difficult to land. And so dangerous. He had tirelessly tried to nail it for over a decade, suffering through broken ribs and concussions. And he'd lost enough teeth to make the tooth fairy go broke.

Now perched 22 feet up on top of the halfpipe, he scanned the electric crowd. He felt the rush of energy and thought 'Today's the day'. On his first few runs he bailed out. Didn't feel right. When he finally tried to land it, he fell forward but wasn't hurt. He started to worry. 'Could this be the ultimate disappointment? What if I can't do it?' On the next run he went too far the other way and fell back. 'Okay, let's split the difference' he thought. He dropped onto the ramp, down one side then up the other. Gaining some height, like jumping on a trampoline. Then he went for it. The crowd edged closer. The other competitors chewed their fingernails. Hawk flew into the air and spun. Once, twice....

But let's back up for a minute. How did the skinny kid from California get up on that ramp in the first place?

Get comfy and let me tell you all about it.

Growing up in San Diego in the early 80's, skateboarding was lame. Kids who walked around with skateboards got picked on. A teenage Tony Hawk liked skating to school, but a block before he got there, he would hide his board in some bushes. He preferred to make himself invisible in the school halls and stay out of the way of the bullies. It worked most of the time.

Hawk played all the team sports that people expected. Football, baseball, basketball - the usual. But he never felt like he was getting any better and never felt excited about playing. Then when he was nine years old his older brother Steve changed his life. He gave him a blue fiberglass Bahne skateboard. Hawk's eyes sparkled and he felt a little flutter of excitement in his stomach. He knew this was a special moment, but he didn't know why.

It was a slow start. "The first time I picked up a skateboard, I ran into the fence because I didn't know how to turn," he laughs at the memory.

But it didn't take him long to get the hang of it. And unlike other sports, every time he went out on the half-pipe he felt like he was learning something new, and that maybe he was kind of good at it. That feeling kept him on his skateboard for hours and hours, trying out new tricks and flips. Long after the other kids had gone home.

Back then, nobody dreamed of being a professional skateboarder. Why would they? They had never heard of one.

Skateboarding wasn't on TV and with no internet back then, it was hard for Hawk to find any role models to look up to or to try to copy. He never thought further than just doing something new and fun the next time he caught some air on the half-pipe.

"I never wrote a script for myself. I was just thinking, 'I want to learn that trick'."

But skating got a little more popular in the early '80s thanks to the success of movements like the Zephyr skateboard team in southern California and movies like Back to The Future where the main character skated everywhere.

By the time he turned 12, Hawk could do some impressive tricks and he started getting noticed by more people in the skateboarding world. He even got sponsored with some free Dogtown skateboards. By age 14 he'd turned pro and was skating in competitions for money.

Hawk was lucky that he had a lot of support from his parents. Not everyone does. They were just happy to see him doing something that he loved. And noticing that the skateboard world needed some organizing if it was going to develop, Hawk's dad Frank helped to create the National Skateboard Association (NSA).

"He would drive me to every skate event in Southern California when I was growing up, and eventually formed the NSA by convincing the fractured & struggling skate companies to work together on a professional competition series" remembers Hawk.

With the help of the NSA and more money flowing in

from clothing and skateboard brands, the sport grew. There were more competitions being held around the U.S. and Hawk went to as many as he could.

And he won pretty much all the competitions he entered. Though Hawk was an accomplished street skater, his reputation came from his skills as a "vert" (vertical) skater, and it was on the half-pipe that he dominated. From battling it out in competitions he quickly learned that his advantage came from doing technical tricks, high in the air, which the other guys just couldn't do. He was fearless. He liked to get as high as he could, dreaming of flying in the sky with the birds. After all, he was a Hawk.

By 16 he was the best competitive skateboarder on earth and had a long line of companies fighting to sponsor him. During the 1980s and '90s, he couldn't be beaten. He won 73 titles and was named the top vert skater every year from 1984 to 1996. And he was still having a lot of fun, coming up with dozens of funny sounding new moves, like the ollie-to-Indy, the gymnast plant, the frontside 540-rodeo flip, and the Saran wrap.

By his senior year in high school, Hawk had made enough money to buy a new house for his family. The funny and sad thing was that when he came back to school after winning yet another competition, he was still just the 'skater boy' that the jocks liked to pick on.

And even on the skateboard circuit, where he was winning, things weren't always easy and happy. Because Hawk was so dominant he didn't have a big group of friends. Nobody likes being beaten all the time. And the other skaters would make fun of him because his dad was in charge of the NSA and was at all the events. And the friends that he did have told him that they knew they were only ever competing for second place. That made Hawk feel a bit lonely. The outsider in a sport for outsiders. Because he was so good, he even noticed that the judges would score him differently to the others. To do well, he didn't just have to be better than the other skaters, he had to be better than himself. In warm-ups he had to hide new tricks from the judges so that they wouldn't penalize him if he didn't perform the trick in the competition.

And things got worse for Hawk after his dad passed away from lung cancer. Though he did live long enough to see how skateboarding was finally making a splash in the mainstream of sports.

Looking back, Hawk says "My dad's crowning achievement came when he saw me on ESPN at the first Extreme Games in 1995; to see skateboarding featured on the sports network he watched most was as big as it could get. He passed away that summer in '95 having no idea about the meteoric rise in store for skateboarding - and my career - that was about to happen."

It was around this time that skateboarding exploded, like a firecracker on the Fourth of July. The TV station ESPN had noticed the rise in popularity of extreme sports like skateboarding, BMX, motocross, skiing and snowboarding. To take advantage of the growing interest they created the 'Extreme Games' to bring all the best athletes together. Then they put it on TV and kids went nuts for it. Hawk competed in the first Extreme Games – later simply called the 'X Games' – and won gold. Now he wasn't just a star in the skateboarding world. He was a star all over the globe.

The first PlayStation came out in America at the same time. And over the next few years different companies asked Hawk if they could make a skateboarding video game with him. He turned the first approach down because their game wasn't much fun to play. But when a company called Activision showed him their game, he loved it. It was more instinctive and fun for non-skaters. He signed up and it didn't take long before there was a lot of buzz in the skateboard world about an awesome new video game that was about to be launched. And the timing couldn't have been better.

Remember where we left Hawk earlier? The crowd urging him on. Praying with everything they had, that he would pull off the 900?

Well, Hawk made fall after fall. He dripped in sweat. One more attempt. And on his twelfth jump he … nailed it! The commentator jumped out of his seat and screamed "Are you kidding me!!!" Hawk raised two arms to the sky before the other skaters stormed the half pipe and raised him up in the air. They clapped him on the back and even harder on his helmet, excited to have been there to witness such an epic moment.

News of Hawks 900 traveled fast across the sporting world. The timing was perfect to introduce the Tony Hawk's Pro Skater video game series. The series became insanely popular making over $1.4 billion in sales across PlayStation, Nintendo 64 and Dreamcast. It was one of the most successful video game series ever made. It created a whole new fanbase for skateboarding, inspiring a new generation at a time when skateboarding was struggling. And made Hawk a very rich man!

Tony Hawk retired from competitive skateboarding after landing his 900. He turned his energy in another direction. Hawk has been sent thousands of emails from parents and children across America who did not have a safe, legal place to skate. Sometimes they were even arrested for skating on public property. Hawk decided to start a nonprofit organization whose mission would be to serve the next generation of skateboarders. He wanted to help communities build safe places to practice and to give back to the sport that gave him so much.

So, in 2002 he used some of the money he had made and started the Tony Hawk Foundation. Over the past 20 years, Hawk's foundation- now rebranded as The Skatepark Project - has helped build over 600 skate parks across the USA.

Hawk recognizes the importance of having a place where misfits can come together and pursue their love for skateboarding. The years he struggled through feeling like an outsider made him determined to offer opportunities to kids who may feel different or excluded. So the next time you feel like you don't belong, think of Tony Hawk.

Now a little older, Hawk isn't catching too much big air, but can still be found some days down at his favorite skatepark in Vans Huntington Beach showing the next generation of skateboarders how it's done.

YUSRA MARDINI

Yusra's father was a professional swimmer. When she was little they would cuddle together on the couch to watch the Olympics on TV. He would point out his favorite swimmers and tell her stories of his own racing days. He was her hero and she wanted to be just like him. She loved it when he would joke that maybe he would watch her on TV someday. Swimming for Syria.

But when the chaos of war came to Yusra Mardini's home in Damascus, her childhood dreams must have seemed like distant stars in a stormy sky. If she was going to be an Olympian, she was going to have to do something special.

Yusra could swim before she could even walk. But it wasn't until she was nine years old that she started training in a group for the first time. She quickly developed into a strong swimmer and as she reached her teenage years she was one of the best swimmers in Damascus. At swim meets she would slice through the water like a knife, leaving the other girls to battle it out for second place.

But her country was in turmoil. Many Syrians were

unhappy about the lack of jobs and the corrupt politicians that ran the country. A civil war started as different groups of Syrians came together to fight against the government.

As the fighting got worse, her dreams collided with the harsh realities of war. "We went to school, but it was dangerous; it was the same with swimming" she recalls. "Our house was destroyed, so we had to live with my grandma, and sometimes with my aunt." All this when she was still only thirteen.

With each passing day the hope of surviving the war at home got smaller and smaller. Their family couldn't go with them, but they urged Yusra and her sister Sara to get far away from Syria so they could be safe. Europe looked like the best bet. They scoured Facebook to find smugglers who were taking people by land into Turkey and then bringing them onward to Greece by boat. Check it out on a map. It's a long way for a couple of teenagers to travel alone. It was going to be a dangerous 25-day journey for the sisters. It was a tough decision for them, they had to leave behind everything & everyone they knew. They were sad and scared, and they couldn't hide their tears as they jumped into the truck with the smugglers. But they had no other options.

"We had to risk everything for our basic human rights and start a new life. It was really hard for me, because I was abandoning everything: our belongings, my family, my friends, my home, everything" Yusra remembers.

After crossing the border to Turkey they were taken down to a jetty, where a small boat crammed with nearly twenty people was waiting. Frightened families clinging together looked up at them as they stepped down into the boat. The sisters squeezed into a little space as the engine quietly puttered out into the bay.

They were nearly halfway along their journey when the engine began to sputter and die. The boat began to drift with the current and it looked like they could be swept out into the Aegean Sea. Being strong swimmers, Yusra, Sara and two others jumped into the water to try to guide the boat in the right direction. They struggled for hours in the water, driven by the fear of returning to Turkey or of everyone on the boat drowning at sea. "Honestly, I wasn't thinking about anything, I was just trying to survive and to save myself and everyone on the boat," she says. "In the moment, you're just thinking about the simple stuff."

Eventually their struggle in the water ended when they made it to shore on the Greek island of Lesbos. At this point they hadn't eaten or drank in days and were very weak. Yusra and Sara collapsed on the shore, exhausted but relieved. There was a restaurant near the beach where they landed. They begged for help but were turned away. Eventually a woman in the street saw them and took pity. She bought them food then got help from the Greek government who looked after them.

But Greece was not where the sisters planned to stay. When they were well enough and they were legally allowed to go, Yusra and Sara continued their epic journey to Germany where the government had agreed to help people escaping from Syria. They were given a place to live and were sent to school. This new world felt very strange to the girls. A different language, different weather, different food. "I didn't really accept living in Germany at first because I thought I would be there only for a while, and then we could go back home when the war ended," says Yusra. They longed to be tucked up in their own beds in Damascus, looking up at the familiar posters on their wall, under the same roof as their family. But the war meant that couldn't happen.

But one thing that did feel just like home was swimming. Once they jumped in the water to swim a few laps, it was as if they were back in the local swimming pool near their home. The Wasserfreunde Spandau club allowed the girls to train there and it wasn't long before a swim coach, Sven Spannekrabs (great name!), spotted Yusra's talents. Sven took her under his wing and trained her just as her father had. During her escape from the war, Yusra had found new levels of courage and resilience she never knew she had. She now poured all this into her training, determined to be the best swimmer she could be.

Because of all the conflict and wars in the world (not just in Syria), a huge number of athletes just like Yusra had to leave their homes. Because of this the Olympic committee had decided that at the next Olympic Games there should be a first ever Refugee Olympic Team.

In a statement about the Refugee Olympic Team, the International Olympic Committee President Thomas Bach said: "These refugees have no home, no team, no flag, no national anthem. We will offer them a home in the Olympic Village together with all the athletes of the world. The Olympic anthem will be played in their honor and the Olympic flag will lead them into the Olympic Stadium. This will be a symbol of hope for all the refugees in our world and will make the world better aware of the size of this crisis. It is also a signal to the international community that refugees are our fellow human beings and are an enrichment to society. These refugee athletes will show the world that despite the awful tragedies that they have faced, anyone can contribute to society through their talent, skills and strength of the human spirit."

This team would be made up of athletes from many different countries who were forced to leave their homes and could no longer compete under their own national colors. Yusra wanted to be part of this amazing new team.

Yusra's coach always told her "Talent is just a small part, it can make the way easier but it's more important to be mentally in good shape and to understand what you want to do and what you want to achieve." Yusra understood. She knew that she had the determination needed to put in the hard work. She trained ten times a week in the pool and another five times a week in the gym. She was exhausted but focused. At the time she said, "I think anything is possible for me because we are working hard, and we know what is our plan... here I have a lot of support (in Berlin) and I think I can do whatever I want to."

Because of Yusra's perseverance and determination in the water, at the age of seventeen she was picked for the team and went to the Rio Olympics in 2016.

Yusra was thrilled with the chance to become an Olympian, just like she had dreamed while sitting on the couch with her dad, many years before. But she had always hoped it would be for Syria she would swim.

Yusra hadn't yet gotten used to the idea that she was a refugee. It seemed like a strange word to her. Before the war the word refugee was only something she had heard on the news, and her image in her mind of a refugee didn't match how she felt about herself. She didn't want to be called a refugee. But slowly she realized that being a refugee was not something to be ashamed of. Nobody chooses to be forced out of their country because of the fear of war. In fact, being a refugee and fighting for a better life takes a lot of bravery and determination. "Now, the word 'refugee' means so many things to me. In the beginning, I was in denial of it. But then I realized that it's just a word, and it doesn't matter what the word means. I am who I am." says Yusra.

The very first Refugee Olympic Team (R.O.T.) was made up of ten athletes from South Sudan, Ethiopia, the Democratic Republic of the Congo, and of course Syria. At the opening ceremony, the team were given the honor of marching with the Olympic flag in front of the host nation Brazil. They were front and center with all the cameras on them. The athletes were a symbol of hope for refugees worldwide and brought global attention to the size of the refugee crisis.

When Yusra arrived at the Olympic village, she was nervous when she saw some of the famous swimmers from countries like the USA and Australia. But her nerves melted away as she thought about how important it was to represent other people just like her who no longer had a country of their own. "It made me proud, and it made me realize I have a voice that I can use to help people understand that refugees are normal people, who have hopes and dreams." Yusra didn't win any medals. But it didn't matter. For her, it wasn't just about competing, it was about stepping out of the shadow and shining a light on the stories of refugees all over the world.

After the Olympics, Yusra was asked to become an ambassador for the United Nations High Commissioner for Refugees (UNHCR). The UNHCR is an organization that works hard to protect people forced to flee their homes. And they help them find a safe place to call home. As an ambassador, Yusra has worked hard to make sure the world knows the heartbreaking stories of refugees across the world. The more people that know about it, the more people will help.

She has visited refugee camps to hear the stories of other refugees. And she has spoken at the World Economic Forum, Google Zeitgeist, WE Day and the Global Women's Forum so that she can share these stories along with her own.

And what's the best way to tell a story to millions of people? By making a movie! Netflix asked if they could make a movie about her and her journey. To help them make it, she had to revisit a lot of the emotions she had felt when escaping from Syria. She found it difficult.

"You don't wake up every day and think about what happened in your life. But then when we saw it on the screen for two hours, it was a very emotional thing to watch," she explains. "But this movie tells the story of millions of refugees all around the world, it's not just my story."

Netflix called the movie 'The Swimmers' after her and her sister. It has been watched all over the world and has helped viewers understand more about the horrible experiences that refugees have to go through.

Yusra credits swimming with teaching her life lessons that she has used to survive and to become a strong confident woman.

"Swimming has taught me a lot: it has taught me patience; it has taught me to know when to ask for help; it saved my life," Yusra says. "Most of all, it taught me to try again. If you're going through something tough, it doesn't mean that it is over."

If you are struggling in sport or outside of it, think of Yusra. Be patient, ask for help and try again. Who knows, maybe we will watch a movie about you on Netflix someday!

LAIRD HAMILTON

Laird looked out at the incoming swell and shouted to Darrick "this is it man, this is the one!" Darrick gunned the jet-ski and towed Laird behind him on his surfboard. Once he had enough speed, Laird let go of the tow-rope and surfed into the barrel of a wave so huge and outrageous that it affected the course of big wave surfing history. He carved his way down the wave, the South Pacific Ocean rose up behind him like a blue wall, curving over and crashing down. So heavy it sounded like thunder. A huge foam ball exploded out the side of the wave and covered him completely. Four seconds later, out of the foamy whiteness, rode Laird Hamilton, somehow calm and steady on a wave seven stories high.

This was one of the most amazing and significant rides in surfing history because it changed what people thought was possible in surfing. A photo of Laird riding the wave on that day August 17th, 2000 was published on the cover of Surfer Magazine with the caption "oh my god…".

The 'Wave of the Millenium' broke 3000 miles south of

Maui on the French-Polynesian island of Tahiti, at a reef pass known simply as Teahupo'o (sometimes pronounced Chow-Poo). Unlike other big surf breaks around the world, Teahupo'o breaks onto a razor-sharp shallow reef, making it one of the scariest waves ever surfed.

When he got back to Hawai'i, his dad asked him "Laird, why do you ride waves like this?" He just replied "I've trained my whole life for this. I don't want to miss an opportunity like that. I don't want to live half a life."

Do you want to know what made Hamilton into such a daredevil? Well let me tell you.

While many surfers like to claim they were "born to surf", Laird was literally born in saltwater. The local University hospital in San Francisco was experimenting with having babies born into salt-water baths and Laird's mom signed up for it. Born in March 1964, even his zodiac sign Pisces uses the symbol of a fish.

Soon after he was born, Laird's dad abandoned them to join the Merchant Marines. And while Laird was still a toddler, his mother decided to move to Hawai'i for a fresh start in life. In the heart of Kauai, Hawai'i, Hamilton's journey began to unfold against a backdrop of adversity, triumph, and the relentless pursuit of passion.

Laird was jumping from 60 ft cliffs into water by the time he was just seven years old. He had a reckless fixation with dangerous challenges. This partly came from the anger he felt from the bullying he suffered. He was fair-skinned blonde boy in Hawai'i and was taunted by other kids for being white. They often called him a 'haole', a derogatory Hawai'ian term for foreigners, - especially white people. Looking back on his childhood, Laird remembers thinking "Well if I do something stupid and people think that it's bad, I don't actually care because you already don't like me because of the way I was born".

While still a small kid hanging out at the beach with friends, Laird befriended a local surfer and surfboard-shaper named Bill Hamilton. Bill took Laird under his wing and taught him how to surf and understand the ocean. Laird brought Bill home to meet his mom, Joann. They hit it off and were eventually married, and Bill became Laird's adoptive father. Laird joked after that he picked his own dad. However Bill had a stormy temper which cast shadows over Laird's childhood. The waves, however, became Laird's refuge, a sanctuary where the turbulent currents of his home life could be left behind.

As Hamilton got older, the waves got bigger. But he didn't just see himself as a surfer. He tried everything he could - swimming, boogie boarding, and bodysurfing kept him entertained. But he needed something for those windy days and unbearable flat spells that arrived during summer. He tried windsurfing and found the fun in it. Of course, Laird threw himself headfirst into this new sport and went on to set speed records and win international competitions. When he got bored of that he went in search again and discovered kitesurfing on a trip to France. He brought home a kite in his suitcase. And despite smashing himself into cliffs and getting stuck in trees, he loved it and helped to make it popular in Hawai'i and beyond. But Laird always considered himself a waterman with a surfer heart. "Surfing on a wave, feeling its power and the freedom that it brings you, is at the heart of my existence as a waterman. I come back to it, over and over again".

Hamilton's experiments with wind and kite surfing sparked his interest in trying new and innovative ways of surfing. First with big wave surfing, he and his friends, known as the Strapped Crew (because their feet were strapped into their surfboards), were the first to use a jet-ski to tow a surfer onto the wave. The jet-ski was needed because no surfer could paddle fast enough to catch the bigger waves. At first they were mocked, but the laughing stopped when people saw the huge waves Hamilton was catching. "The world doesn't need more conformists. If you don't fit in, celebrate that, and then get ready to stand your ground," Laird said, reflecting on the lessons learned in those early struggles.

Laird once read a famous quote from Thomas Edison which said, "To be an inventor all you need is imagination and a pile of junk". Laird had heard of something called a hydrofoil, which was used on boats to lift them out of the water and make them faster. He had a pile of junk in his garage and his imagination made him wonder what would happen if he attached a hydrofoil to his surfboard? His workshop looked like a mad scientist's laboratory as he worked out the best way to do it. He tried different sizes, different materials and different positions. But his hard work paid off. When he finally got it in the water it looked like a flying surfboard! He was pretty stoked and the foil board was born.

There was no end to Hamilton's energy and passion for life.

I bet you've heard of Stand-Up Paddle-Boarding, or SUP for short? In Waikiki in the 1940s, older surfers would use a canoe paddle to help them keep their balance while surfing. Fast forward fifty years and Laird, along with his friend Dave Kalama, started doing the same thing just for fun. But this time they started making extra-long and flat boards that were better for standing on. And once people around the world started seeing videos of Laird 'surfing' with his SUP, it quickly became one of the fastest growing sports in the world.

Laird's journey through life wasn't just about conquering waves but about pushing boundaries and inspiring change. "A little adrenaline every day keeps the boredom away," is one of his favorite sayings. And his life seemed to embody this philosophy.

If he wasn't surfing, he was fighting against offshore drilling and doing his best to protect the ocean.

But some of his biggest challenges have been in dealing with himself. His quest to live life to the extreme often made life hard for him.

He broke his ankle learning to kite-surf and many times felt like his lungs would explode while he was pinned to the ocean floor after yet another wipeout from a huge wave.

And he often broke his wife's heart by heading off on another adventure and leaving her at home to worry if he'd come back alive. It nearly ended their marriage. "Make sure your worst enemy doesn't live between your own two ears," he advises, knowing that the battles with your own thoughts and anxieties can be as challenging as the thundering waves.

Laird Hamilton made his way through the unpredictable currents of life and emerged triumphant. He's maybe the closest thing to a superhero on a surfboard. Especially when flying through the air on his hydrofoil.

And he has shown that as long as you're willing to learn, there's an endless supply of knowledge. The world is an amazing place, but you just need to go and explore it. Laird did and found his passion. What's yours? It's okay if you don't know. Just keep exploring.

GORDIE HOWE

The snow was just starting to thaw in the fields of Saskatchewan. The meltwater ran into the rivers and filled them, ready to burst. The geese hadn't yet returned from their migration down south, but the melted ponds meant the ducks were happier. It was around this time in the spring of 1928 that the hockey gods sprinkled a little fairy dust over a small farmhouse at the edge of town. Under the leaking roof, Gordie Howe entered the world. The best hockey player ever had just been born.

Would you like to hear more about him?

Gordie's childhood came against the backdrop of the Great Depression. This was a time when there were not enough jobs to go around, and families couldn't make much money. Many people in the United States and Canada were living in poverty. Even though his parents Ab and Katherine worked hard, it was difficult to protect and provide for their nine children. That was a lot of mouths to feed, a lot of backs to put clothes on.

Despite his parents' best efforts, Gordie often heard the

rumblings of hunger from his belly. At dinner his mom would dish the food on to their plates, and he would quietly pray for an extra spoonful. But they never had any. This meant that Gordie was often sick as a child. Doctors feared that he wasn't getting enough calcium because his spine looked slightly curved. To battle this, they told him to drink as much milk as he could and to do chin-ups to improve his strength and straighten his back. Gordie was a good patient and did as he was told. His parents gave up their milk so he could get enough. Slowly his health improved, and he was able to get back to playing games with other kids in the neighborhood.

When Gordie was five years old, a neighbor donated a bag of clothes to his family. Gordie dived headfirst into the rucksack to see what was in it. Right at the bottom of the bag was an old pair of ice-skates. Gordie's eyes twinkled at the marvelous things he held in his hands. Once he put them on, he never wanted to take them off again. Even though he had to share the skates with his sister! Luckily for him, she wasn't that interested in skating.

In Saskatoon where Gordie now lived, hockey was the sport that everyone loved and talked about. Once he got the hang of skating and after many falls on the ice and many a wet and bruised backside, Gordie made his first attempts at using a hockey stick. At first, he just used it to help him balance, but before long he was pushing a puck around the ice. And as he got better and better his love for hockey blossomed on the frozen ponds near his home.

As the Great Depression cast its shadow, young Gordie made the tough decision to leave school to help support his family. He went to work with his dad as a laborer on construction sites. The work made him strong, but it was hard for a young boy when all he wanted was to play hockey with his friends.

On days where the work was getting too much for him, Gordie wondered if he would be doing this for the rest of his life. The thought made him sad. But his passion for hockey was a guiding light and brought a lot of joy into his life. In his own words "I knew what it was to be hungry, but I didn't know what it was not to have a hockey stick." Every chance he could get, he was out on the ice.

Gordie immersed himself in hockey. He played day in and day out throughout the year, using a puck, a tennis ball, or even clumps of dirt. Despite his early battle with illness, Gordie had grown to be bigger than many of his friends but was a bit clumsy when he skated. He didn't make it the first time he tried out for the local hockey team. But Gordie was determined and spent hours and hours skating by himself, practicing turning, twisting, starting and stopping. By the time his twelfth birthday rolled around, Gordie was a far more fluid skater and was showing a lot of promise. His skills with the hockey stick had grown too, and he could make the puck dance to whatever tune he played.

After a few years of starring for his local team and showing himself as one of the best players in the league, he caught the eye of the professional scouts. When he was fifteen, the New York Rangers invited him to a tryout camp. The camp director, though, was unimpressed. He felt Gordie didn't have what it would take to make it in the major leagues. But Gordie was used to overcoming challenges and he didn't let this rejection deter him. He went back to the ice and worked harder than ever. Eventually his determination helped him to land a tryout with the Detroit Red Wings. Jack Adams was the coach and general manager of the team and he was excited by the potential he could see in young Gordie and signed him to the team straight away.

Gordie settled in well at Detroit and soon found himself on the starting team. His hard work in training impressed his teammates and his toughness in the tackle made him a fan favorite. However Gordie's career almost came to an abrupt end. Detroit was having a really good season and made the playoffs. In the first playoff game against the Toronto Maple Leafs, Gordie collided with Toronto's Ted Kennedy and flew headfirst into the sideboards. His skull was fractured, and he suffered a concussion. He also smashed his cheekbone and broke his nose. In the hospital, surgeons had to operate to relieve the pressure on his brain as it began to swell up. He was in critical condition for days and there was a risk that he might not survive. But the doctors had done a good job and Gordie pulled through. When he woke up Gordie was advised by the surgeon that he shouldn't play hockey again, because another bad bang on his head could kill him. But Gordie couldn't face the prospect of giving up hockey. As soon as he was out of the hospital he started back training, slowly at first but it wasn't long before he was going into full contact tackles with teammates. He made some changes to his helmet to give him some extra padding and was raring to go when the new season rolled around.

But the question was, would he still have the same fire and grit that he had before? Gordie answered that question by playing in every game that season and leading the National Hockey League (NHL) in goals, assists and total points. He never backed out of a challenge and played the game harder than ever.

In the world of hockey, you have to be tough just to get on the ice. And Gordie Howe showed that he was as tough as old boots. Many had doubted his return, but Gordie's resilience won out. Reflecting on that challenging time, he once said, "You find that you have peace of mind and can enjoy yourself, get more sleep, and rest when you know that it was a one hundred percent effort that you gave." These words sum up the spirit of a true champion who refused to be sidelined by adversity.

Gordie's skills on the ice were nothing short of extraordinary. His powerful shots, control of the puck, and physical prowess earned him the nickname "Mr. Hockey." Others liked to call him "Mr. Elbows" because of the way he protected the puck. With his skill and speed to go along with his size, Gordie transformed the role of a power forward and raised the bar for all the other forwards in the league. His style of play was the perfect combination of skill and brawn.

His approach to hockey inspired the coining of the "Gordie Howe hat-trick". A player earns this if he gets a goal, an assist and a fight all in the one game! Funnily enough, Gordie himself only did this twice in his long career. He often got a goal and an assist, but most players tried to stay out of his way and were smart enough not to start a fight with him!

But Gordie Howe's impact extended far beyond just toughness & resilience. Over a professional career that spanned five decades, he became renowned for his goal-scoring prowess, breaking records and leaving a lasting mark on the sport.

Scoring an impressive 801 career goals in the NHL, Gordie Howe set a standard that few have matched. His goal-scoring ability, combined with his playmaking skills, made him an unstoppable force on the ice. He won six Hart Trophies as the NHL's Most Valuable Player (MVP). He also led the NHL in playoff points six times and he holds the record for the most seasons played (26) in the NHL. He sure proved those doctors wrong.

And Gordie's success wasn't limited to individual achievements either. He loved to assist teammates and help make others around him play even better. At training he set the standards that the rest of the team tried to match. Gordie and his team at the Detroit Red Wings went down in history as one of the greatest ever after they won four Stanley Cups in 1950, '52, '54 and '55. His leadership and skill played a pivotal role in these victories, making him a hero in the hockey world especially in Detroit.

When Gordie eventually retired in 1971, it didn't take long before he was inducted into the Hockey Hall of Fame. But as it turns out his playing career wasn't over.

Gordie's phone rang and he got up to answer it. There were no cell phones in those days. It was his son Mark. He talked so fast that Gordie could barely understand him. "Dad, Marty and me have just signed for the Houston Aeros. But they're short a power forward. We said that you still had it in you. And they want you to join too. We could all play together. Imagine that!"

In a rare and heartwarming family tale, Gordie had the joy of playing professional hockey with his sons, Mark and Marty. Although now in his mid-forties, the 'old man' showed them how it was done. He scored over 100 points twice in six years, won two straight championships in 1974 and 1975, and was even named the MVP in 1974. This unique story added another layer to his legendary career. It showed not only his individual greatness but also his role as a supportive and inspiring father. As Gordie once put it, "I played a hundred games with my sons, and it was the highlight of my whole career."

Behind the scenes, his wife Colleen Howe, lovingly known as "Mrs. Hockey," was essential to Gordie's success. Her unwavering support and management of the business side of his career allowed him to focus on what he did best – playing hockey. As Gordie pointed out, "Colleen was the most important person in my hockey career. She was the one who made sure everything ran smoothly." Their partnership was a testament to the strength of their bond and the crucial role supportive relationships play in achieving greatness.

Gordie Howe eventually retired again at the age of 52. He was the most durable hockey player of all time, going on to become the only player to have competed in the NHL in five different decades.

Gordie's story goes beyond statistics and records; it is a tale of triumph over adversity and a celebration of resilience. In the hearts of those who watched him play, Gordie Howe remains more than just a hockey legend. He is a beacon of hope and determination.

Gordie's journey from the challenges of the Great Depression to hockey greatness, teaches us that hard work, perseverance, and a passion for what we do, can help us overcome huge obstacles and shape our lives to match our dreams.

KATHRINE SWITZER

Once upon a time, in the bustling town of Amberg, Germany, a determined and adventurous little soul named Kathrine Switzer was born. The snow was falling outside the hospital window as her mom swaddled her in a soft pink blanket and gently touched her nose, "It might just be because I'm your mom, but I think you're going to be a special little girl" she whispered to her daughter, only a few hours old. But nobody would have guessed that this tiny newborn would grow up to be a trailblazer, shattering stereotypes and breaking barriers for girls all around the world.

Kathrine's dad was a Major in the US Army and when he got his orders to ship out, they left Germany and headed home. She was only a toddler when they settled in the quaint town of Lynchburg, Virginia. Set in the shadow of the Blue Ridge mountains, it was the perfect place to raise a daughter with such an adventurous soul.

Kathrine discovered her love of running almost as soon as she learned to walk. If she was going somewhere, she was running! And as she grew up and could go for a run by herself, she enjoyed jogging along the banks of the James River as it wound its way through the town. She loved the rhythm of her feet pounding the pavement. And the aching feeling in her legs as she rounded the last block and made a sprint for home. She liked to pretend she was charging for the finish line in a big race and would give it all she had before collapsing in her front garden, exhausted but thrilled. Running wasn't just a sport for her. It was a passion, one that would shape her destiny.

Growing up in the 1950's & '60s, it was hard for Kathrine to find a female runner to look up to. This was a time when a lot of people thought that running was only for boys. And that was only a small taste of the discrimination that women and girls had to put up with. Can you imagine that in the '60s a woman couldn't open a bank account without her husband? Women weren't allowed into Ivy League schools like Harvard, Yale and Princeton. Even the leader of the country, President Kennedy, went on TV and said that the primary responsibility of women was in the home. So, in the '60s the USA was sending men to the moon but an unmarried woman couldn't go to the bank and get a credit card.

But Kathrine was not one to be held back. With determination in her heart, she laced up her sneakers and raced toward her goals, breaking through the notion that certain sports were off-limits for girls.

All through high-school Kathrine was a tough competitor on the road and on the track. After graduating she went to Lynchburg College but her hunger to keep improving meant that she eventually transferred to Syracuse where they had a stronger athletics department.

As Kathrine's love for running grew, so did her desire

to push boundaries. She set her sights on a challenge that no woman had ever conquered before – the famous Boston Marathon. In those days, the marathon was considered a man's race, and women were not officially allowed to participate. But Kathrine wasn't one to be discouraged by such outdated rules.

At Syracuse, there wasn't a women's cross-country team, but after pleading her case, Switzer was allowed to join the men's cross-country running program. And it wasn't long before she was pushing her coach, Arnie Briggs, to train her for her first marathon. Briggs had never seen a woman run a marathon and wasn't confident that the distance was right for Switzer. But he told her: "If any woman could do it, you could, but you would have to prove it to me. If you run the distance in practice, I'd be the first to take you to Boston." Switzer took on the challenge and proved Briggs wrong. By the winter of 1967, she was training for the upcoming Boston Marathon, tackling the most difficult running routes she could find on the roads around Syracuse. There were many times when her chest burned from not getting enough air, or her toenails turned black from all the pounding on the road and trails. But the motivation in her heart was so great, she was willing to take any pain that came her way.

At that time the rule book for the Boston Marathon didn't say anything about men and women. It just assumed that all the entrants would be men. But the Amateur Athletic Union (AAU), which oversaw the race, had declared that women could not compete in any race that was longer than a mile and a half.

Before Switzer came along, this rule was already being challenged by other female runners. In 1966, Bobbi Gibb had tried to enter the race officially but had been rejected by the race Director Will Cloney who claimed women were incapable of running 26 miles. Gibb proved him wrong by hiding herself in the bunch of runners at the start line and going on to finish the race ahead of most of the men with an amazing time of 3:21:40. But Gibb was not an official entrant so there was still another hurdle to overcome for women to be treated equally.

With a heart full of courage, Switzer registered for the 1967 Boston Marathon using only her initials, "K.V. Switzer." When the day arrived, Kathrine got suited up in her favorite gray tracksuit and pinned her race number 261 to her jumper. Along with her coach Arnie Briggs and her boyfriend Tom Miller, she stepped out to join the sea of determined runners. Little did she know that this marathon would become a historic moment in the fight for women's rights.

The organizers didn't know that a woman was among the athletes and were shocked when Kathrine appeared on the course. In a moment that would define her legacy, the race manager Jock Semple tried to forcibly remove her from the race. But Kathrine stood her ground, refusing to be sidelined.

Recalling that pivotal moment, Kathrine later said, "I got off that truck, and my coach, Arnie, shouted to the official, 'This is a girl. Now leave her alone'."

But that didn't stop the race manager from attacking her, "I jerked my head around quickly and looked square into the most vicious face I'd ever seen. A big man, a huge man, with bared teeth was set to pounce, and before I could react, he grabbed my shoulder and flung me back, screaming, 'Get the hell out of my race and give me those numbers!'"

Semple's attack knocked off one of Switzer's gloves, but not her race number. And when Switzer's slightly built

50-year-old coach Arnie Briggs tried to protect Switzer, Semple knocked him to the ground. But Switzer's boyfriend competed as a hammer-thrower and was a big guy. He put his shoulder into Semple knocking him back, where he stumbled and fell.

Switzer was shaken by the attack. But her determination only got stronger in the face of adversity. She continued running, fueled by the idea that she was not just running for herself but for every girl who dreamt of breaking free from society's unfair rules. Her grit and resilience made her the first woman to officially complete the Boston Marathon.

Switzer finished the race in just over 4 hours and 20 minutes. Semple's attack was captured by photographers and the incident was seen in newspapers and on TV all over the world. And even though Bobbi Gibb had run the marathon also (finishing almost an hour ahead of Switzer), it was Switzer's courage in officially entering the race and confronting the man who attacked her, that brought the most hope to other female runners.

The aftermath of Switzer's historic run sparked a revolution. Women around the world were inspired to lace up their sneakers and hit the roads. The barriers that once held them back began to crumble, thanks to the fearless spirit of Kathrine Switzer. But it didn't happen overnight.

Because of what she had done, the AAU banned women from competing in races against men. It took another five years before the Boston Marathon created an official women's race. After this, other races began to open to women, and soon all AAU races had entries for men and women.

Reflecting on her journey, Kathrine shared, "People thought that I was too weak and fragile to run 26.2 miles. That moment when the official attacked me, I realized that I had the strength not just to run a marathon but to challenge the status quo."

Kathrine Switzer's boldness didn't just help female runners; it lit a match under the rocket of gender equality in all sports. Her legacy lives on in every woman who crosses a finish line, proving that no dream is too big and no hurdle is too high.

Jock Semple, the race manager who attacked her, was the villain of this story. But a few years after the race, Semple apologized and unbelievably, the two became friends.

Switzer remembers. "I realized Jock Semple was just an overworked race director protecting his event from people he thought were not serious about running. Sure, he was notorious for his bad temper. And, sure, he was a product of his time and thought women shouldn't be running marathons. But I wanted to prove him wrong on that point. So it was really Jock who gave me the inspiration to create more running opportunities for women. Almost every day of my life I thank him for attacking me, because he gave me this spark. Plus, he gave the world one of the most galvanizing photos in the women's rights movement. Sometimes the worst things in your life can become the best things." Switzer had a skill for taking the biggest challenges and turning them into great opportunities.

Since that amazing day in 1967, she has worked to improve running opportunities for women. And in 2011 she was inducted into the National Women's Hall of Fame for creating a social revolution by empowering women around the world through running.

But she also had some personal glory on the road. She was the women's winner of the 1974 New York City Marathon, one of the biggest marathons in the world. And fittingly she set her personal best marathon time at the Boston Marathon in 1975, a lightning fast 2:51:37.

Switzer was named Female Runner of the Decade (1967–77) by Runner's World Magazine. Even after she retired from running competitively, she enjoyed commentating on TV when there was a big marathon on. Her first job was the 1984 Olympic women's marathon in Los Angeles. And she did such an amazing job that she won an Emmy Award!

In a world full of challenges, remember that you too have the power to break barriers. Kathrine Switzer's footsteps echo through time, encouraging us all to run with bravery, resilience, and the unshakeable belief that anything is possible.

GERAINT THOMAS

You might think that a cyclist who has won Olympic gold and conquered the Tour de France, would have grown up dreaming of cycling glory. Not Geraint Thomas. He was just a regular kid trying out every sport under the sun until something stuck. And it just happened to be cycling. Luckily he was pretty good at it.

Thomas hails from Cardiff, Wales. A city where rugby reigns supreme. Geraint was your typical sports-loving kid. He kicked around a soccer ball, dodged tackles on the rugby field, and even took a dip in the pool now and then. Drying off after a swim one day at the Maindy Leisure Center, he saw an advert for the Maindy Flyers, a local cycling club on the hunt for new recruits. He figured, "Why not give it a shot?" and before he knew it he was away racing on weekends.

Thomas describes it; "I just enjoyed the whole social side of it, really. I was still playing rugby and a bit of football but then, as I got older, the knocks in the rugby started to hurt a bit more and I just went to swimming and cycling." Thomas started to get pretty good at swimming and the coaches wanted him to go in the mornings before school. But it only took a few cold mornings, dragging himself out of bed before he soon said, "No, I'm alright. I don't want to get up at half-five!". His dad was pretty happy too because he didn't like getting up that early either to drop Geraint to training.

Soccer too had dropped away – strangely Thomas wasn't a fan of being kicked in the shins. And then all that was left was cycling.

It probably helped that he was showing a lot of promise in the saddle. "I was winning local bike races and I knew I was pretty good, but just on a local scale. We did start going over to the rest of the UK and racing on weekends, and I started winning those races, but it wasn't really until I was a junior, under-19, when I won the Worlds and won quite a big race in France. That's when I really thought, "I can make a living out of this".

Up until that point, it was more just people saying to me, "You've got a talent", but it's one thing believing it and another thing actually doing it. Once I won the Worlds, I really started to believe, and I knew I could achieve bigger and better things.

With a mix of self-belief and hard work, it wasn't long before Thomas found himself pedaling for Great Britain (Team GB) at the Olympics.

If you don't know much about cycling, it can be confusing because there are many different types. With track cycling the cyclists are big and powerful and blast in circles around a wooden track called a velodrome. They go so fast they almost become a blur, like remote-controlled cars on a toy track. Then there's road cycling where the cyclists are usually smaller and skinny so they can be light enough to climb over big mountains. Like mountain goats on shiny bikes.

It was on the road that Thomas first made his mark. After joining a French team in 2007, he was picked to compete in that year's Tour de France, the most prestigious and grueling bike race in the world. Over 200 cyclists come from all over the world to compete. The race is around 2,200 miles long, goes over huge mountains and takes over three weeks to finish. Thomas was the youngest rider in the race and was worried that he might not be strong enough.

Many riders start 'Le Tour' but never make it to the finish line. There are so many people in the race that the cyclists often bunch together in groups of around 50. The noise from their bikes can be deafening as they speed together down the hills. And if two cyclist's wheels bump into each other, all the bikes come crashing down like a row of dominos. Sometimes when there is a big smash the cyclists end up piled on top of each other like a box of jigsaw pieces. So, it was a huge achievement for Thomas to make it through the race, a stronger and more experienced rider.

It was even more impressive then when he decided he wanted to compete on the track in the 2008 Olympics in Beijing. He had to change his training to try and transform himself from skinny mountain goat to explosive race car.

But would he be able to do it in time?

He sure would! Thomas was picked to be part of the 'team pursuit' event, where four riders from each team race around the track. Team GB made the final where they beat Denmark to the gold medal. They even set a new world record. The commentator joked that they were so fast their wheels might catch fire. And four years later, Thomas and his team defended their title, making him the proud holder of two Olympic gold medals.

But it wasn't always blue skies for Thomas. Even though they might look small and skinny, cyclists are known for being some of the toughest and most daring competitors in sport. In some races, they can speed down hills at 65mph and don't have anything to protect them except a helmet. Next time you're in the car with your family, peek at the speedometer and see when it gets to 65mph. Then picture yourself on a bike!

Thomas has had his share of accidents.

Back in 2005, he was training with the British Team in Sydney, Australia. The cyclist in front of him clipped a bit of metal debris and it flew up into his spokes and locked his front wheel. Thomas flew into the air. He bashed himself off his handlebars and then bounced off the ground. He was hurt. He was taken to hospital where the doctors told him, "You've ruptured your spleen, and if it keeps bleeding we're going to have to take it out or you're going to die". "Well what are you waiting for, then? Take it out!" Thomas told them. "Well, it's stopped now, but we're monitoring you and if it starts again, then we'll take it out."

Eventually, at two o'clock in the morning, he was woken up by the doctors and they operated on him to remove it. The surgery left Thomas with a big scar all the way down his chest. In interviews he has recounted how it was a pretty scary time for him, especially as it happened on the other side of the world so far away from family and friends.

But British Cycling flew his mum, dad and brother to Sydney, so they were with him when he came out of hospital. But he couldn't wait to get back on his bike. To the amazement of the doctors he recovered to win a bronze medal at the Commonwealth Games the following year.

But do you think that was the end of his bad luck?

A few years later, he was coming down a mountain in Italy. Descending on his time trial bike, he overshot a corner, went a bit too fast and went over the side. He dropped down about twenty feet onto the road below. He landed so hard that he fractured his pelvis, broke his wrist and scraped all the skin on his backside. "The pelvis didn't take too long to heal, really, because it was only a fracture; it wasn't completely broken, and I could still hobble around on crutches. My hand took a bit longer because, at first, they missed it. So, it was about two months later, and it was still really swollen and giving me a bit of grief, so I had that operated on. I had a bone graft and a pin, and, by the end of 2009, I was fully recovered and racing again and did the Manchester World Cup where we won the team pursuit and the individuals."

Injuries like this would be enough to make most athletes think 'Hang on, should I really be doing this? Do I need to put my life on the line every time I go out training?' It's a question that Thomas has pondered.

"What made me go on? I don't know. I just don't know anything else. I just love riding my bike and when they tell you you've got to have this amount of time off the bike, you're gutted because you just want to be riding all the time. It's never a case of, 'I won't be able to ride again', it's just, 'When can I ride again?'. I couldn't imagine not being able to ride."

That grit, determination and pure love for cycling paid off for Thomas. By 2018 he was part of Team Sky who were aiming for victory in the Tour de France. Chris Froome was the team leader and was hoping for his fifth Tour win. The team strategy was for Thomas and their other teammates to support Froome during the race. But that plan went out the window early on when Froome had a bad crash. He was still in the race but was too far back to challenge for the win. The team looked to Thomas, but he didn't know if he had what it took to be the leader.

Stage 12 of the race finished at the top Alpe d'Huez. The climb is known for being super steep and one of the most difficult in cycling. With just a few hundred meters to the finish line, Thomas was in the leading group. "It's now or never" he thought. He stood out of his saddle to power his bike up the hill and at the finish line he threw his bike forward to try and get his wheel in front. He won by inches. And he was now winning the overall race. It was a proud moment for Thomas when he pulled on the famous yellow jersey that is reserved for the race leader. Thomas rode as hard as he could and held onto that jersey with all the strength he had. When he was certain that he couldn't be caught, Thomas and his Team Sky teammates celebrated as they rode along the Champs-Elysees in Paris. Even taking time to sip a glass of champagne as they cycled.

Since that win, Thomas has had glory in other races but has never been able to repeat his Olympic wins or Tour de France victory. But his philosophy on sport might not be what you would expect from somebody so competitive.

"We all get caught up about winning Olympic medals but, when you sit back and look at it, there's so much more to life than an Olympic medal. It's really good to keep that in perspective. We're so lucky to do what we do, all sportsmen, all professional sportsmen. I think we can get so wrapped up in this whole, 'What if I don't win?', or 'I've just come second. I only got a silver'. It's not really that big when it comes to it, really, is it?"

Thomas' approach to cycling has meant that he still enjoys it after all the struggles he has been through. He has overcome horrible accidents and injuries that would put an end to most athletes' careers. But the setbacks and the external pressure to be the best hasn't taken the fun out of it. "I just enjoy riding my bike," he says. Sometimes it's as simple as that.

BILL RUSSELL

It was Game 7 of the finals and the Boston Celtics were trailing the St. Louis Hawks by two points. It was winner takes all. Up to now it had been one of the best games ever played. The teams had dunked, jumped and run until they were exhausted. The crowd were going crazy. Stomping their feet and whooping and hollering as loud as they could. It felt like the excitement on the last day of school. They knew they were witnessing something special.

But there had to be a winner.

"We're not losing, not on my watch" thought Bill as the sweat dripped off his nose. He grabbed the ball and with just a few seconds left on the clock he made a sweeping left-handed layup to tie the game. Then he chased down Jack Coleman from the Hawks, and leaped high to block his shot just before the buzzer went. The amazing last-minute play by Russell tied the game and, two overtimes later the Celtics were the 1957 NBA champions. The 23-year-old Russell had just won a championship in his first season and given the world a taste of what was to come.

William 'Bill' Russell grew up in West Monroe, Louisiana along the banks of the Ouachita River. The town was strictly segregated, and the Russell's struggled with racism. Young Bill often saw both his mother and father treated with disrespect for no other reason than the color of their skin.

After World War II began, word got out that there were jobs available in the shipyards of Oakland, California. The Russell family packed up and headed west. They settled in the Oakland projects, where Bill went to McClymonds High School. But when he was only 12 years old, Bill's mom died after a brief illness. He had been really close with his mom, and her death affected him badly. He lost his confidence and didn't want to be around his friends and family. He just wanted to be alone and would disappear for hours to go reading by himself in the Oakland Public Library. He liked to lose himself in all the amazing stories he could find and forget about his own life for a while.

Bill's father was a trucker and was away a lot. But he went out and found a new job as a steelworker so that he could be at home more to see his kids. He thought that playing sports might help Bill deal with his grief. And he was right. After his first basketball session Bill couldn't stop talking, "Dad, at the start I kept missing but then the coach told me to move my hands and then I made two baskets and then I passed to Tommy and he made a basket as well. Can I go back next week?". Russell had found basketball, and never looked back.

When he started in high school, Russell was 5'10". He showed promise in track but couldn't make the basketball team. But by senior year, he'd sprouted to 6'5". Though he was still awkward on the court, his height gave him an advantage and encouraged him to keep playing.

And even as his body was still growing, Russell had already started to use his greatest weapon to reimagine the game - his mind. It may sound strange now, but until the 1950s, the thinking about basketball defense had been that a defender should stay on the ground and not jump. If he left his feet, an offensive player could drive by him and draw a foul.

Russell began to experiment by jumping to block shots. Even though his coaches tried to stop him at first, he kept at it and started to see that this new, airborne style could completely disrupt an opposing team's offense.

During Russell's senior year, a scout from the University of San Francisco (USF) came to one of his games to check out another player. Russell was just beginning to bring it all together on the court. With his new smothering defensive style, nearly every time the other team shot, he would intercept it like a dog catching a frisbee. And at the same time he hit his high school scoring record of 14 points.

It was enough for him to be given a scholarship to USF, the only one that was offered to him. But it was all he needed.

Russell could see that university was a chance to escape from the racism and poverty he'd grown up with. He enrolled in 1952 as a freshman and, over the next decade, spearheaded what can be considered the invention of modern basketball.

At USF, Russell's talents exploded. He grew to nearly 6'10" and had to buy wooly socks to keep his feet warm at night because they stuck so far out of the bed. His new coaches helped him refine his style of aggressive defense. He perfected the art of swatting away shots, challenging shooters, pulling down rebounds, tossing out passes and dominating the key. He was fierce and he defended the ring like a grizzly bear defending her cubs.

In his junior year of college, the USF Dons went 28-

1. They won the Final Four, Russell was a First Team All-American and he averaged 20 points and 20 rebounds, and a lot of blocked shots which they didn't count at the time. And the cherry on top came when he was named the NCAA Tournaments Most Outstanding Player. But, at the Northern California sports banquet, they picked another guy as Player of the Year - a white center whose numbers were not nearly as good as Russell's. Bill had left West Monroe but couldn't escape the racism. He was deeply hurt by this but didn't let it keep him down. Instead, he used it to make him stronger. Russell said he learned then that black players could be cheated out of individual awards, so he decided to focus on what was in his control—making his team win.

Russel led USF to another championship in 1956 and was snapped up by the Boston Celtics in the draft. This marked the start of a magical era for the Celtics, with Russell inspiring his team to an incredible 11 championships in his 13 years in the league!

Russell, of course, would never claim that he won those championships – the Celtics won them. He was a team player who took pride in doing the hard work that wasn't always noticed. He wasn't the one making dunks just so his picture would be in the newspaper. Russell once wrote, "The most important measure of how good a game I played was how much better I'd made my teammates play." Even opponents seemed to notice how nice it looked to play with Russell - he was named the regular-season MVP five times during the era in which the award was picked by all the players in the league.

Now standing at 6'10" (2.08 m) tall, with a 7'4" (2.24 m) arm span, Russell was a blocking and rebounding machine. His arms were so long, and he moved so fast, he was like an octopus who could play basketball. He played in a time before 'Defensive Player of the Year' awards existed. They didn't even record blocks and steals back then. But it's safe to say he would have won a few. He led the NBA in rebounds four times, had a dozen seasons of over 1,000 rebounds, and is the second of all-time in both total rebounds and rebounds per game. Along with his rival Wilt Chamberlain they are the only players to have grabbed more than 50 rebounds in a single game. That's a lot of rebounds. And during the final three seasons of his career (1966–1969), he was the player-coach of the Celtics, making him the first black NBA coach to win a championship.

But Russell's success didn't protect him from the same issues facing black people in the rest of the country. When he joined the NBA there were still only about 15 black men playing in the League. The Celtics had drafted a black player before named Chuck Cooper, but when Bill arrived in Boston, he was the only black person on a team of white men. Russell—as well as other black NBA stars such as Wilt Chamberlain, Oscar Robertson and Elgin Baylor—was making his mark in the NBA just as the United States was entering the Civil Rights era.

The surge of the Civil Rights movement placed black athletes—some of the most visible African Americans in the country—into the political spotlight. Muhammad Ali was banned from boxing for three-and-a-half years after he refused to enter the army when he was drafted. On the medal stand at the 1968 Mexico City Olympics, runners Tommie Smith and John Carlos held their gloved fists above their heads in Black Power salutes. Russell, in the meantime, forged his own way - outspoken, opinionated, uncompromising and thoughtful.

He was at the 1963 'March on Washington for Jobs and Freedom'. He was in the front row of the crowd to hear the Rev. Dr. Martin Luther King Jr. deliver his famous "I Have a Dream" speech. And after the assassination of civil rights leader Medgar Evers, Russell traveled to Jackson, Mississippi to lead the first ever integrated basketball camp in the state's history. He was also front and center supporting Muhammad Ali when he refused to be drafted during the Vietnam War.

Russell felt the sharp knife of racism throughout his career, even in Boston, the city he brought so much glory to. Vandals once broke into his Massachusetts home and covered the walls with racist graffiti. But such hateful treatment never stopped Russell from taking a stand against the injustices around him. In 1961 in Lexington, Kentucky, a restaurant wouldn't seat Russell and his black Celtics teammates before an exhibition game. Up to now black athletes had been expected to put up with such discrimination. But Russell and his teammates made the brave decision to boycott the game. Russell felt that with great power came great responsibility. And he felt responsible to do his best for the black community.

He spoke up against injustices and inequality on a regular basis, both in the world of sport and beyond it. To him, he was doing what he thought was right and fair. But to spectators and critics, he was an arrogant, uppity, self-important athlete, even though he was just fighting for fair treatment.

In 1969, as player-coach, Russell won one last title with the Celtics before retiring. Russell is the winningest player in NBA history with 11 NBA championships, including eight consecutive titles from 1959 to 1966. It's hard to believe that his record will ever be broken.

By the time he retired, professional basketball had been

transformed from a ground-based game to one played in the air and above the rim. And the NBA had gone from a league with 15 African American players to one that was mostly black.

Russell, over the years, transformed as well. From a childhood of rural poverty in Louisiana, he'd pushed himself to become a champion and an international superstar.

But as dazzling as he was on the court, it's his courage and impact on the Civil Rights Movement that inspired former President Barack Obama to give him the Presidential Medal of Freedom in 2011.

Bill Russell stood for the values of equality, respect, and inclusion. And he stamped these values into the DNA of the NBA. Bill rose above the taunts and threats and remained true to his belief that everyone deserves to be treated with dignity.

On and off the court he fought hard to help and elevate those around him, to make their game and their lives better. When Russell had started playing basketball, both black players and black Americans were expected to stand in the shadows. By the time he was done, they had emerged.

MELISSA STOCKWELL

Meet Melissa Stockwell, a true-blue American from Grand Haven, Michigan. A woman with Olympic dreams that took an unexpected turn. Growing up, she dreamed of being a gymnast, picturing herself flipping her way to the podium. Little did she know that her Olympic journey would lead her down a very different path, one that she could never have imagined.

Melissa was from a very patriotic family and was a proud American. After graduating from the University of Colorado she felt compelled to sign up for the army. She felt that she had a calling to represent her country on the battlefield. She was commissioned in March 2004 as a Second Lieutenant, and soon found herself deployed in Baghdad, Iraq with the 1st Cavalry Division.

Barely a month later, cruising through central Baghdad in a routine convoy, her Humvee drove under a bridge. Then all she heard was a massive BOOM! It was a roadside bomb. The Humvee was blown up and her whole life changed at that moment.

Stockwell often recalls how she woke up that morning with two legs but went to bed with only one. Her left leg was badly injured in the blast and had to be amputated above the knee. She had the unwanted record of being the first American female soldier to lose a limb in active combat. But Stockwell looked around her hospital room that night at some of the other patients. Most were in a lot worse shape than her. Ever the optimist, she saw herself as lucky — she still had her life and three good limbs. She was only 24 and had a lot of livin' to do. Right then, she decided to make her life one of triumph, not regret.

But it wasn't going to be easy.

Walter Reed Army Medical Center became her new home. After many surgeries, infections, and countless other hurdles, she took her first steps on a prosthetic leg. She felt like a newborn foal trying to walk on ice. But it was a start. She remembered the famous saying "A walk of a thousand miles starts with a single step". Her first step was a pivotal moment that fueled her determination to be more than 'just' a survivor.

But she couldn't do it alone.

Thanks to organizations like the Wounded Warrior Project, Achilles' Freedom team, and the Challenged Athletes Foundation, Melissa not only rediscovered her athleticism but pushed boundaries she could never have imagined. Skiing down Breckenridge in Vale, Colorado on one leg and hand cycling the New York City marathon were just the beginning. She learned to swim, to bike and to run again. "I learned to take the opportunities presented to me and, most importantly, to believe in myself again" she recalls.

In 2005, John Register from the Paralympic Military and Veteran Program opened her eyes to the Paralympic Games

— the world's second-biggest sporting event. Stockwell had been medically retired from the Army after being awarded a Purple Heart and a Bronze Star for courage. What was the next chapter of her life going to look like? How about becoming a Paralympian and representing the country she defended in Iraq? Stockwell set her sights on Beijing 2008 and went to work on turning her dream into a reality.

Swimming was a major part of her rehabilitation work at the hospital. She loved the water because it made her feel whole again. Just floating made her forget she was missing her leg.

Stockwell joined her first competitive swim team and learned to love the smell of chlorine. Slowly her times improved. When U.S. Paralympic Trials came around in April 2008, she was a long shot to make the team. But knowing that hard work pays off and that dreams really can come true, she just went for it. She had the meet of her life when it mattered most and was named to the 2008 U.S. Paralympic Swim team. Stockwell became the first Iraq War Veteran to qualify for the Paralympics. She even had the honor of carrying the American flag in the Beijing closing ceremonies.

But her journey didn't end there.

Stockwell had discovered Paratriathlon, a race where the athlete has to swim, then bike, then run to the finish line. She was bitten by the bug and decided that this was going to be the sport for her. She earned her stripes as a three-time World Champion in the TRI2 division (the sports in the Paralympics are broken into different divisions based on the level of an athlete's ability). Her commitment to training meant that it wasn't long before she was named the female Paratriathlete of the year and went on to win a bronze medal in the Rio 2016 Paralympic games in Brazil. As the national anthem played, Stockwell stood on the podium next to her USA teammates who had won the gold and silver. She gazed up at the Stars-and-Stripes and felt grateful for all the amazing people that had helped her to get there.

In 2019 Melissa and her family moved to Colorado Springs so that she could pursue her dream of making it to the Tokyo Paralympics in 2020. Colorado is popular with endurance athletes because of all the training opportunities it provides at high altitude. But Stockwell, being the ambitious and caring person she is, also had dreams outside of sport.

After her leg was amputated, Stockwell tried out many different prosthetic legs. At first, they were uncomfortable and hard to use. But over time and with the help of her medical team she was able to adapt them to suit her particular needs. Every person, and every amputee is different. Even just taking Melissa as the example, she uses a different prosthetic leg for walking, another for cycling and another for running.

Stockwell's experiences made her think that maybe she could help others with their prosthetic journey. She went back to school to do the prosthetic practitioner program at Century College in Minnesota. Here she learned to design and fit artificial limbs for other amputees.

And soon Melissa and her husband Brian Tolsma, made the dream of owning their own prosthetic practice a reality and Tolsma/Stockwell Prosthetics (TSP) was born.

TSP opened its doors in early 2020 and helps many elite level athletes who are preparing for the Paralympic Games. They also help adults and children in the local community. This change in career is a great example of how Stockwell kept turning setbacks into opportunities to help and inspire people.

Stockwell's move to Colorado paid off and she qualified for the games in Tokyo (which were delayed to 2021 because of the Covid pandemic).

Training and taking part in sports has been at the center of Stockwell's recovery. Sport gave her particular goals to work towards and helped her regain her confidence as she began to make her way in the world as an amputee. With this in mind, Stockwell and some friends founded 'Dare2tri'. This is a not-for-profit paratriathlon club. Their mission is to enhance the lives of people with physical disabilities and visual impairments. They do this by building confidence, community, health and wellness through swimming, biking, and running. Despite all her athletic accomplishments, Stockwell looks at this as one of the achievements she values the most.

"I think the legacy you leave behind is inspiring the next generation. Maybe there's a 10-year-old girl who just lost her leg and doesn't know what she can do with her life, and she turns on the TV or looks at her phone and says: 'Oh, look at this girl, she's just like me. If she can do that, I can do it as well'" she says.

Stockwell is a three-time Paralympian, a wounded veteran, a mom and an inspirational speaker. She has done more with one leg than most people will ever do with two.

As Melissa says, "Life is too short. You might as well do the things you want to do. Don't wait for tomorrow to do them. You should do them now."

If we can learn anything from Stockwell, it's that sport can help us in ways we could never imagine. And helping others achieve their dreams can be as rewarding as achieving your own.

TOM BRADY

When people think of Tom Brady, what comes to mind are words like 'champion', 'talented' & 'legend'. The word 'adversity' and Brady usually don't go together in the same sentence. But as the great man Benjamin Franklin once said, "out of adversity comes opportunity."

But what kind of adversity could the amazing Tom Brady have had?

Before the G.O.A.T. (greatest of all time) was throwing touchdown passes and winning Super Bowls in the NFL, he was just a kid from San Mateo playing ball in the street.

Growing up, life revolved around playing sports. Whether it was football, baseball, capture-the-flag or just riding bikes around the block, the group of neighborhood kids on Portola Drive usually could be found outside. And even though it was all fun and games to most, no one took their contests more seriously than Brady.

"Even then, he was the most competitive kid out there," remembers his childhood friend Scott Cannel. "He hated to lose. He hated to strike out. He hated to misthrow somebody.

It was kind of funny to see how competitive he was then, to how competitive he is now."

Baseball had its own set of neighborhood rules. A fire hydrant marked the pitcher's mound, home plate was a manhole cover. If the ball hit a power line, it was a do-over. Hitting the ball past the big tree on the corner meant a glorious home run. What could be better?

They broke windows, lots of them. There were even a few broken bones, but they had a lot of fun. And the parents on the block didn't mind too much, they just thought "At least the kids are outside playing. They're not in trouble."

When they played baseball, Brady would smash tennis balls over the neighbor's houses with his booming swing. And when they played football in the park, he was one of the younger kids in the group so didn't get to play quarterback or receiver. But he was so competitive he would scream for the ball and tackle as hard as anyone. He just always wanted to be involved.

During high school, Tom was getting more attention in baseball and was drafted as a catcher by the Montreal Expos. But Tom's heart was in football. Growing up in San Mateo, he was a die-hard 49ers fan, and his dream was to be a quarterback like his hero Joe Montana. When Brady was six years old, all the kids got dressed up for Halloween. Most were dressed as vampires and scary monsters of some sort. But not Brady. He went trick-or-treating in full 49ers uniform, number 16 like his hero, even wore the helmet.

Brady ended up committing to the University of Michigan to play football and enrolled in the fall of 1995. Tom redshirted (when a student-athlete sits out for a playing season, but still keeps their four-year eligibility) his first year and did not see any game time until his second year.

But 1996 would be different.

In September, UCLA came to town. The Michigan Wolverines were mauling the visitors 35–3 and the game was nearly over. Coach Carr saw a chance to give Brady a few minutes on the field. Brady, the 3rd string quarterback took the field for his first experience of college football. But he was nervous. His body felt tight. He was breathing heavily. Then he made his first play. And his first ever pass attempt was the worst thing that could happen. He throws a 'pick 6', an interception returned for a touchdown by UCLA worth 6 points. It was the only touchdown UCLA would score in that game. It was a horrible start for Brady, and it would be a while before he got a chance to redeem himself.

Despite the initial set-back, Brady trained hard, and the following year was rewarded by being promoted to back-up quarterback. Michigan won the National Championship that year, with Brian Griese starring at quarterback. Brady didn't get on the field much and only threw 15 passes the entire season. It looked like a move away from Michigan might be the only option for Brady to get a starting place. But his competitive nature meant that he wanted to stay and fight for his spot.

Brady went to work on improving his training, researching what all the top pros were doing, and worked hard to copy them. He got bigger, stronger and faster. But it was the growth in his mindset that had the biggest impact. Brady credits Michigan sports psychologist, Greg Harden, as a key in helping him get to the next level. "Greg came into my life at just an incredible moment," Brady said in an interview with The Detroit News. "Obviously, I had moved from California to Ann Arbor choosing to go to school in Michigan. It was a lot of tough competition and I really had to grow up. I think

Greg recognized the state of mind where I was thinking, 'Is there an easier path for me?' Greg helped me realize that the path that was best for me was to learn how to take on the obstacles I was facing and to do the best that I could."

Tom's dedication and patience paid off and he became the starting QB the following year. But Michigan had a disappointing start, losing their first two games against Notre Dame and Syracuse. Brady was under pressure. Then late in the Syracuse game, he was benched and replaced by the talented freshman Drew Henson. Brady could never make the spot his own and the two quarterbacks split playing time over the next two seasons. Because he had never established himself as the number one quarterback at Michigan, all 31 NFL teams passed on him in the early rounds of the 2000 NFL draft. But he was eventually selected by the New England Patriots with the 199th pick in the 6th round. When his name was called out, he whooped and hollered with his friends and family. He was off to the NFL.

But he still had a lot to do.

Brady started both the 2000 and 2001 season as the backup to Drew Bledsoe. It did take a little bit of luck for Brady to become the starting QB in New England. Bledsoe got injured after a rough hit by Jets linebacker Mo Lewis in game two of the 2001 season. Suddenly, Brady was the starter. It was coming together for him.

Brady had a fantastic season and led the Patriots to their first ever Super Bowl victory over the Rams. Every pass he threw was like a laser guided missile, exploding with the roar from the crowd, cheering another touchdown. His decision to face his obstacles had paid off. It was an amazing accomplishment for the then underdog Brady who went from 199th draft pick to Super Bowl Champion in less than two years.

The next season, the Patriots traded a now healthy Drew Bledsoe to Buffalo and decided to hold onto Brady. That turned out to be a pretty good decision. In 2003 & 2004 the Patriots would go on to win back-to-back Super Bowl championships with Brady leading them. He was like the conductor of a beautiful orchestra, helping his team-mates hit the right notes at the right time, creating a beautiful melody. Brady went on to win a record 6 Super Bowls with New England before joining the Tampa Bay Buccaneers for his final season. He signed off in style by lifting yet another Vince Lombardi trophy.

Brady had a tough start to his career. He didn't do all that well in university and it took an injury to give him a game at New England. But Brady says that's probably why he did so well in the end. "The challenges I think toughened me up a lot. Growing up in California, and then going to Michigan and competing with those guys for as long as I did, it was a great experience. I took a lot of those things that I learned in university and brought them to the professional level. I was lucky to learn a lot of lessons at 19 and 20 and 21 that a lot of guys don't learn until they're 23 or 24 or later when it's too late."

Tom Brady has shown that it takes a lot more than just talent to succeed. Perseverance, a bit of luck, and confronting his challenges are what has made him the greatest QB of all time. Will anyone ever win more Superbowl Rings than Brady? If they do, it won't just be because of talent, that's for sure.

JILLION POTTER

Jillion just sat staring at the doctor. She was in shock. Once she heard him say the word 'cancer' she zoned out. He was still talking but she couldn't take it in. She stared around the room. On the doctor's desk she saw a photo of him and his family smiling. The kids were on swings being pushed by their parents. She started to think of all the experiences she might miss out on if this cancer beat her.

She didn't cry at first. It wasn't until she picked up the phone to tell her mom that the news really hit her. She found this one of the hardest things about the diagnosis, having to tell the people who loved her the most.

Jillion had always thought her biggest challenges were on the sports field. But all that was about to change.

But what's so amazing about Jillion Potter? Well, let me tell you.

The smell of fireworks was still fresh in the air when Jillion Potter and her twin brother Paul were born on the fifth of July 1986 in Austin, Texas. When Jillion was a teenager her parents Scott & Vikki moved them to Albuquerque, New

Mexico because they could get better jobs there. Jillion was nervous about starting at a new school. Fitting in and finding new friends. Would they like her? Or would they make fun of her for being a 'Texas gal'? As she took her first steps through the halls of La Cueva High School, she saw the school motto written on the wall in huge blue letters "La Cueva - where excellence is a habit". Luckily Jilion had a habit of being excellent. At least on the sports field. She signed up to all the sports teams and quickly became a standout athlete for the La Cueva Bears. She loved running out onto the field to the sound of the school cheer 'Let's go Bad Bears!' When it came time for graduation she didn't want to leave New Mexico. She loved being close to her family and friends. So when she graduated Jillion chose to go study at the University of New Mexico which was close by.

It was here that she fell in love with a sport she barely even knew existed. "A couple of girls came up to me and said: 'Hey you! Do you want to come and play rugby?'" she recalls. "I didn't even know what rugby was, but then it happened again the next day, and the next day. I thought I had headhunters or something."

Potter's first taste of the action was a tackling and running session – and that got her hooked. She enjoyed the smash of the tackle and fire in her lungs when she sprinted down the field. Even when she was the one being slammed to the ground, she would wipe the dirt from her face, get back up and think 'Awesome, what a buzz!'

"I didn't realize how physical I could be. I got knocked down by this girl, and I thought, 'Oh, this is how it's going to be. Let's go!' And I stuck with it."

At the end of her first practice she strolled off the field smiling and chatting with her new teammates and thought,

'This is the sport for me'.

And Potter soon found that her new sport came with a big bonus. Rugby came with a big new community of friends and like-minded people. She loved it.

But during those early days of playing, she never believed that rugby could become a career. "I had no idea there was a USA team," she recalls. "But about six months into my collegiate career, my coach was adamant that I should go on a USA under-19 developmental tour. Then I made the under-19 team, was recruited to the under-23 team, and it just went from there."

But that could have been the end of it.

In the buildup for the 2010 World Cup, Jillion played in a game against Canada. After a tackle she landed awkwardly. When she tried to get up she couldn't move. She couldn't feel her arms and legs and was stretchered off the field to hospital. There they told her she had broken her neck and she might have trouble walking again. But Potter defied the odds. Once she had surgery, it looked like she would be okay to walk. Her next fear was that she would never be able to play rugby again. But she remembered her school motto "excellence is a habit". She turned her rehab into a habit, repeating her exercises over and over. Day in day out. After a year of amazingly hard work, she was back on the pitch. And it wasn't much longer before she was again wearing the red, white and blue of the USA Eagles rugby team.

Sevens Rugby is a shorter form of rugby which features teams of 7 players instead of the usual 15. Only the fastest and fittest players get invited to be on the team. Jillion joined the Sevens team and quickly became their captain. Despite having broken her neck, she played harder than ever. Jillion earned the reputation as a strong and powerful player. She would hunt down opposition players like a cheetah after a gazelle. Her teammates nicknamed her "The Dominator" and "The Enforcer" and she quickly became one of the world's top rugby players.

But her journey doesn't stop there.

With life and rugby seemingly going well, Potter was brushing her teeth one morning when she noticed swelling underneath her jaw. This was right at the start of the Rugby World Cup and the worst possible time to get ill. But she didn't think it was anything serious.

"I had been to Alaska with my wife Carol, and we went camping and did outdoor things," she says. "And I thought maybe I had got something from being in the wilderness and let it go, thinking it was an infection."

She took antibiotics but the problem didn't go away. Then doctors discovered a tumor, but a scan appeared to show it was benign. The doctors gave Potter the all-clear to keep playing at the World Cup. She was relieved and played every game in the tournament. But the tumor continued to grow and started affecting her speech because it was pushing up on her tongue. Eventually she was diagnosed with a rare form of cancer called Stage 3 synovial sarcoma.

Back in the doctor's office staring at that picture on his desk of him and his family, she thought "I'm going to do whatever I need to beat this". Potter had shown that she was a fighter on and off the field. This time would be no different. She was quick to focus on what lay ahead. "Once we had that diagnosis and we had a plan, we knew what we needed to do in terms of treatment," Potter said.

She quickly started her treatment of chemotherapy and radiotherapy. Because of the treatment Potter started to lose her hair and she eventually shaved her head. "I felt like an alien after I lost my eyelashes," she remembers. The rugby community rallied around her. Her teammates gave her a lot of support and started a fundraising campaign that raised thousands of dollars to help with her medical costs. She also got loads of messages of support from rugby players across the world who she would normally have thought of as being her rivals. Even from women she had smashed to the ground in rugby matches. It made her smile. But she missed being around her teammates.

"Through the whole ordeal, I thought about rugby and how I wanted to come back. The biggest thing I had to do was to remind myself to be patient. And being okay with where I was right in that moment. Because you can't beat yourself up. Of course you have your ups and downs and your doubts and your fears. But you really just have to keep moving forward and have a positive approach" she said.

The medication made Potter feel ill and she had a lot of bad days. But even then, she would think about helping others. Some well-meaning friends brought her board games and puzzles to help pass time in the hospital. But a lot of the games were more suited to children. So Potter came up with the idea to walk them over to the nearby Children's Hospital, making the journey while connected to her IV pole.

It also helped her get through this difficult period by knowing that Sevens Rugby had been added to the Rio Olympics as a new sport. This gave her extra motivation to stay active during her treatment. Even on the days when she was getting treatment, instead of sitting with her IV drip in her arm, she would walk 3 miles around the hospital to try and stay active, wheeling the IV pole next to her.

After a few months the cancer was gone, and the doctors gave her the green light to get back to rugby. Once she was fit enough, she joined back up with USA rugby and captained the team as she made her comeback at the Rugby Sevens tournament in Dubai.

Nine months later, she proudly played all six matches as rugby returned to the Olympic Games in Rio, where the USA finished fifth. But Potter was diagnosed with cancer for a second time at the start of 2017. Rugby gave her the values and drive to get through the treatment. She said "When you get tackled, you always have to get up off the ground. Just like life". She beat the cancer for a second time.

Jillion has always remarked how the experiences she gained from playing rugby helped her battle her cancer.

"I'm just grateful to be here. Rugby teaches values and those values are what really prepare you for life. It's the values that you learn on the pitch and off the field that really set you up to overcome challenges. Rugby has given me a wonderful gift and it has taught me a lot about mental toughness & discipline and hard work and integrity. All those things really play a role in how I beat cancer."

Because of how she handled herself on and off the field, Jillion had earned a lot of respect. She was the first person given the Leadership Development Scholarship which was awarded to inspiring female leaders across World Rugby. That same year she served as an assistant referee at the Rugby World Cup Sevens in San Francisco. And then in 2019, she was on the first panel to pick the World Rugby Women's Player-of-the-Year.

Through her positive attitude and amazing resilience, Jillion has shown us that when you get tackled, the most important thing to do is to get back up and keep going.

LUKA MODRIĆ

The crowd went quiet & they all looked towards the stage. For the previous ten years, nobody except Lionel Messi and Cristiano Ronaldo had won the Ballon D'or award for being the best soccer player in the world. Tonight, it looked like it might be eleven years. Then Didier Deschamps announced the winner; "Luukaaaaaaa Moddddddrić!!!" Modrić stepped out through the smoke-filled stage to claim his place amongst the greatest soccer players of all time. This small, skinny boy who escaped war as a refugee. Who everybody said was too small to succeed. Who other players tried to bully. Now crowned as the best in the world. Modrić tried to believe it was true. 'How did I get to this place?' he wondered.

Well, let me tell you how.

Modrić had a sad start to life. When he was still very young, the hills around Modrić's childhood home were occupied by Serbian forces during the Croatian War of Independence.

It was the week before Christmas, 1991, around 9am. A shepherd was out on the dusty road near Modrić's home, looking after his flock of sheep and goats, while they grazed on the dry mountain grass.

While he was working, Serbian soldiers spotted the shepherd and stopped to question him.

"Who are you, what are you doing here? This is Serbian land", they snapped.

The terrified shepherd took a couple of unsteady steps forward, and the soldiers reached for their guns and pointed them at him. A loud crack of a rifle rang out around the mountain and the shepherd fell down dead. He was Luka Modrić's grandfather.

Luka was six years old at the time. The life he had – quiet, rural, helping his beloved grandad in the fields – was over. He was a refugee now, along with his parents and sister. They left and never came back. The soldiers had booby-trapped the area around their house with mines. It was too dangerous to ever live there again.

That was the last childhood home of Luka Modrić. He didn't get another one. Instead he and his family traveled to the nearby town of Zadar, where hotels were being converted to provide rooms for refugees like Luka. The hotels were very crowded, with entire families living in a single room. The Modrić's called the Kolovare Hotel their home for the next seven long years, while the war raged on.

But the Kolovare did have one perk. When Modrić lived in the mountains on the side of a steep hill, he had nowhere to play soccer. The ball would just roll away down the hill. But the Kolovare had a nice flat car park. And lots of other kids to play with. This is where young Luka Modrić began to obsessively hone his football skills. A teacher from his primary school lived opposite the car park and would implore him to go inside and do some homework. Always a polite boy, Luka would say "just a little longer, please?"

Luka loved to try any sport he could. He enjoyed basketball and played two-on-two with some friends, including the future national team goalkeeper Danijel Subasic. Modrić excelled as a goalkeeper himself, in handball.

However, the first time his P.E. teacher Albert Radovnikovic saw him with a football at his feet, he was astonished at how good he was. He would try to challenge him, by making him play against older boys, putting him in goal, or sometimes both. But Modrić would overcome all those challenges and still win.

The children were not always able to use the school gym for those lessons and they weren't even sure that there would be class every day. Zadar was still a war zone, with artillery shells falling regularly in the neighborhood. Luka and his classmates were forced to shelter under their tables when they heard the air-raid sirens.

It was the same story at the local football pitch, where Luka was becoming a force to be reckoned with. There would be occasions at training when the alarms would start to wail, and the teams would have to take cover. When it was all over, they'd come back out to finish their game.

The children at the school were shielded from the worst of the war but it still had an effect. Once in the third grade, Luka was asked to write a story about something which had had an emotional impact on him. He chose to write about the death of his grandfather.

There is scarcely a successful soccer player alive who has not had to overcome one obstacle or other. But the challenges that Luka Modrić had were unique.

He was first raised in a house where he couldn't play football. And the war meant that sport and hobbies took second place to the quest for survival.

And then there was the issue of his size. He was always the smallest and skinniest player on his team. The shirt he wore should have fitted a boy his age but always fitted Luka like an 'extra-large'. But Luka had many other skills that more than made up for his lack of height.

He was rapid across the ground and could cleanly win any kind of challenge. His P.E. teacher would say that he could make a slide tackle on the concrete playground and come up without a scratch on his legs.

His low center of gravity meant he could twist and turn easier than his taller teammates. He played the game, just as he does today. Other habits remain too.

When he first turned professional and joined Dinamo Zagreb, he would come home after a game and sit down to watch the footage of the game he'd just played in. Even if it was late at night after an away game, he would study it closely to see where he could improve for the next game. Those who knew him at Real Madrid say he did exactly the same thing.

At the start of his career Modrić was sent to play in 'the butcher league' in Bosnia to harden him up. But he was tougher than they thought. He was named player of the year there and then returned to Croatia where more incredible performances brought him to the notice of the big clubs in Europe.

In April 2008, Tottenham Hotspur agreed to pay £16.5 million for him to join them in London. This was a record for the club back then.

Modrić had a slow start. He suffered from a knee injury in an early game and some of the newspapers began to say that he was too light-weight to play in the physical Premier League in England. But Modrić's determination and grit shone through and he helped turn 'Spurs' into one of the top teams in the league. Never forgetting about the hotel he was forced to live in for many years, the very first thing he bought with his pay packet was a house for his mother and father, somewhere they could call home again.

His star continued to climb higher when in August 2012, Real Madrid announced they had agreed to pay Tottenham £30 million to bring Modrić to Spain .

At Madrid, Modrić paired up with Cristiano Ronaldo to form one of the most successful teams of all time. Together they won an unmatched five UEFA Champions Leagues to go with his three La Liga and two Copa del Rey medals.

But some of Modrić's favorite footballing memories were made in the red, white and blue of the Croatian national team. He was captain for the 2018 world cup.

The small nation of 4 million people was not expected to get very far in the tournament. But Modrić had different ideas. He put in some of the best performances of his life. He would finish games crippled with cramps because he had run so much and he scored some beautiful goals to help his team make the final against France. Even though they were beaten by France, Modrić was still awarded the Golden Ball for the best player of the tournament.

Slaven Bilic, the Croatian manager, knew how lucky he was to coach Modrić. "Luka ...is a player who makes others better, they all benefit from him being in the team. He's not selfish, he's playing for the team...he's a complete player; good in defense, good in offense – it looks like he was born with the ball at his feet."

After winning games at the World Cup, Croatia celebrated on their team bus with the song "Nije u soldima sve" (Money Isn't Everything). An old Zadar team-mate noticed that it was the same song - by Luka's favorite singer Mladen Grdovic - he used to sing with his youth team in Zadar 20 years earlier. Despite all his success, Modrić really hadn't changed much.

Back at his abandoned childhood home, an admirer has tied a Croatian flag that flutters in the doorway. There are some messages scrawled on it. One says 'Thank you'. Another says 'Our captain Luka'.

Many soccer fans will only know of Modrić from the day he first played for Dinamo Zagreb. But the hardest parts of his career came way before then. Surviving the war, dealing with doubters, making it through the loan spells in the Bosnian league where the other teams would target him and try to kick and injure him. But he would dust himself down and go again the next week.

After receiving the Ballon D'or, Modrić looked over the crowd and spoke into the microphone "this shows that we all can become the best with hard work, dedication, and belief. All dreams can come true."

Modrić dreamt of being the best soccer player in the world. What are your dreams?

DANIEL "RUDY" RUETTIGER

It was the last play in the final game of the season. And the crowd at Notre Dame were going wild. On the field, a 5'6" defensive end had just made a game winning sack on the opposing quarterback, securing a thrilling victory for the Fighting Irish. That tackle marked the highlight of Rudy Ruettiger's unusual college football career.

But how does such a small guy get to pull on the jersey of maybe the most famous college football team in the world?

Daniel "Rudy" Ruettiger's remarkable journey had one roadblock after the next. His family were poor, he was dyslexic and he was a pretty small guy. But he didn't let any of that stop him from becoming a legend among the Fighting Irish.

Born on August 23, 1948, in Joliet, Illinois, Ruettiger grew up on the outskirts of Chicago. He had 13 brothers and sisters. It was a household of hand-me-downs and money struggles. But it was a happy house and with so many siblings he always had someone to play with.

Rudy developed a passion for football through his father,

a hardworking miner and devoted Notre Dame fan. The family's weekly gatherings to watch football brightened Rudy's childhood. And they sparked his lifelong aspiration to one day play for the Notre Dame football team. He had a fire inside of him that no amount of firetrucks could put out.

Gordie Gillespie was voted by the Chicago Tribune as the head coach of the newspaper's 'All-Time Illinois High School Football Team'. And luckily for Rudy he was the coach at his high school. Ruettiger's grades weren't too good, but he was a promising athlete. With the help of Coach Gillespie he developed into a very quick cornerback, making more tackles than anyone on his team. Despite his small frame, his high school success gave him a lot of self-belief and made him even more determined to play for Notre Dame.

However, Ruettiger's size and dyslexia created physical and academic hurdles. He was too small to get a football scholarship and his grades weren't good enough for him to get an academic scholarship. And he didn't have the money to pay his way to Notre Dame. So when he graduated high school, his football dreams felt entirely out of reach. Ruettiger felt that he may as well have been trying to fly to the moon. He didn't know what direction to go next, so he enlisted in the United States Navy. It was 1968 when he shipped off to join the Vietnam War.

Returning home after two tours, Ruettiger was able to claim G.I. Bill benefits. These were payments from the army to help Vietnam veterans pay for college. "Wow, I can finally afford to go to Notre Dame" he thought. Ruettiger applied as soon as he could but was rejected because of his poor high school grades. So instead, he enrolled at Indiana's Holy Cross College. There, he found out that if he got all A's, he could try to transfer to the nearby Notre Dame after only four semesters.

During his time at Holy Cross, Ruettiger discovered that he had dyslexia. It helped explain why he found reading in school so difficult. But now that he knew what dyslexia was, he figured out different ways to study that made it easier for him. Instead of reading all his books, he listened to tapes of them where possible. His grades quickly improved. To pay his way he got a job as a groundskeeper on the nearby Notre Dame campus and slept in a spare room in the basketball arena. And after two years at Holy Cross and after having three disheartening rejections, 'Rudy' Ruettiger was finally accepted and became an official Notre Dame man. When he found out he ran around the empty basketball arena screaming "I did it, I finally did it!" His shouts echoed around the arena. He couldn't believe his dream was finally coming to life.

But he still had a lot of work to do.

When he got to Notre Dame, the first thing Ruettiger did was head to football tryouts in the hope of making the team as a 'walk-on'. That's someone who becomes part of the team without being recruited or given an athletic scholarship.

Ruettiger only weighed 165 lb and was a lot lighter than your average college footballer. The tackling drills were the hardest. He had to face guys nearly twice his size. Every tackle would feel like he was getting smashed by a steam train. But every time he was flattened to the ground like a football pancake he scraped himself up, straightened his helmet and went back for the next tackle.

The coaches could see Ruettiger's determination. And it helped that he was quick and worked harder than anybody else on the field. He soon made the scout team and then graduated to the varsity team.

After the 1974 season, the Notre Dame head coach Parseghian stepped down and former Green Bay Packers coach Dan Devine replaced him. Parseghian liked Ruettiger and had promised him an opportunity to play on the field to reward him for his hard work at training.

But his replacement, Devine, had made no such promise. Ruettiger was frustrated and was anxious because he thought he might go through his whole college career and never get to play even a single minute.

But that was about to change.

It was a cold Saturday in November as Notre Dame battled Georgia Tech. Ruettiger sat with in his uniform watching the game, trying to keep warm. Then he heard his name called by the coach. "Get ready Ruettiger, you're going in". He couldn't believe it. His heart pounded in his chest with excitement. He could hear his pulse thumping in his ears.

Ruettiger missed his first tackle. But on the next play he danced around the blocker and flew through the air at the quarterback. He slammed him to the ground. He'd sacked him and the game was over. They'd won! The crowds roared as Ruettiger's teammates carried him off the field on their shoulders. Not only had Ruettiger's dreams been realized - but he'd become a Notre Dame legend.

After leaving Notre Dame, Ruettigers friends and family encouraged him to try and tell the story of his amazing journey. Ruettiger pitched a film project based on his life story to Hollywood executives. Nobody was interested. But if Rudy had learned anything in university, it's that hard work and persistence pays off. He tracked down a famous screenwriter named Angelo Pizzo. Angelo had written a popular movie called Hoosiers about a high-school basketball team in Indiana that Ruettiger loved. At first Pizzo also had no interest but Ruettiger kept after him and convinced him to write the screenplay. With Pizzo's involvement, everything came together for the movie to be made.

The University of Notre Dame were happy for the movie to be made on their campus because they thought it would be a "heartwarming, enlivening story" about hard work that embodied the school's values.

The most important scene in the movie, where players carry Rudy off the field was shot during that year's Notre Dame vs. Boston College game, with the 59,000 fans present all chanting Rudy's name. Ruettiger sat there listening, remembering the real moment and couldn't believe that he got to do it all again.

When the movie went to theaters, "Rudy" was a hit. The Chicago Sun-Times called it "a small but powerful illustration of the human spirit". Who doesn't love a good underdog story? The movie made Ruettiger famous, spreading his inspiring story throughout the world. He was invited from all around the country to give talks about his experiences and made a new career as a motivational speaker. Ruettiger felt fortunate and wanted to be able to help other players that were like him. So he created the Rudy Foundation which gives out awards to honor Division 1 football players who show what Ruettiger refers to as the Four Cs: character, courage, contribution, and commitment.

So if you think you have a challenge that's too big, remember Rudy Ruettiger and his journey from his boyhood in Illinois to his heroics at Notre Dame and success in Hollywood. It doesn't always matter what size you are, as long as you have a big heart.

KATIE TAYLOR

The bell sounded for the start of the fight. Ding, ding, ding. Persoon exploded from her corner and threw lightning fast punches from all angles. Taylor was forced back into the ropes and was only able to put her arms up to protect herself. She felt a blow to her ribs that took her breath away, then a jab to her eye. But she used her quick feet to dance her way out of the corner, and started throwing some punches of her own. For the next four rounds, Persoon piled on the pressure. Never stopping. Taylor did her best to keep her chin out of the line of fire. The crowd roared and screamed but she didn't even notice. She was only focused on one person.

But Persoon, the tall Belgian, landed a big left-hand that made a cut in Taylors forehead. It swelled up like a golf ball. But Taylor wouldn't give up. First she fought back with her trademark rapid-fire combinations. Jab, jab, hook. Jab, jab, cross. Persoon was getting tired and now her face was looking red and swollen, and her eye was closing up.

As the final bell got closer and closer, the tired fighters dripped in sweat. But nothing would stop them from giving every last ounce of energy they had. They traded punches to try and finish each other off. After the bell rang the two fighters raised their arms in the air, hoping that they had won. As the judges scores were announced, the referee raised the hand of the winner. But who's hand would it be?

Before you find out, let me tell you a bit more about Katie Taylor. So gear up and get ready to hear about a warrior.

Taylor is from Bray, a coastal town just 12 miles south of Dublin, Ireland. The Taylor family didn't have much, as Katie described "We were a very, very poor family living in the roughest area but God chose our family and did something with us. I have two brothers and one sister and we all became successful. But nobody would have looked at our family or our house and thought 'Success will come to them.'"

But one thing the Taylors did have was boxing. Her mother, Bridget, was the first female boxing judge in Ireland and the year Katie was born her father, Pete, was the national light heavyweight champion. When Katie was ten, he opened a boxing club in Bray that would prove pivotal in his daughter's love of boxing. Katie would go to the gym with her father and two brothers and desperately wanted to be involved.

Like many female boxers, nothing came easy. When she was growing up, women's boxing was banned in Ireland. So Katie had to fight just to be allowed into the boxing ring. And because women's boxing was not allowed, there were no other girls for her to fight.

The family's solution was simple but effective. Taylor would pretend she was a boy to get fights. They put her name down just as 'K. Taylor'. And she would pull the headgear on, tuck her hair inside so no one could see it, and then get into the ring that way. When she won and took the headgear off there would be uproar when everyone suddenly saw that she was a girl. Katie won a lot of fights and caused a lot of uproar.

But it wasn't just in boxing where Katie was starting to make her mark. Taylor was a brilliant soccer player and represented the Republic of Ireland women's national team at under-17, under-19 and senior levels. She was 14 when she played for the under-17s and 15 when she started playing for the under-19s. According to Taylor, her boxing training helped her football career because it made her physically strong enough to bridge the age gaps. On an amazing day for Taylor in September 2003, she scored four goals for the Republic of Ireland under-19s in a European Women's Championship qualifier against Macedonia. She went on to play 11 times for Ireland, but the lure of the boxing ring was too strong.

"I did have a chance to get a soccer scholarship over in America when I left school, but boxing was always my number one passion. I knew I had to choose between the two sports and I obviously chose boxing."

The law on women's boxing in Ireland changed in 1997 to allow female boxers compete. But some of the people in charge still didn't like it so it took another four years for an official women's contest to happen in Ireland. When the time finally came for the historic first bout, it was obvious that the young prodigy from Bray should be involved. Taylor's opponent was another promising teenager, Northern Ireland's Alanna Audley-Murphy.

The fight took place at Dublin's National Stadium, a 2000-seater boxing arena. The biggest crowd Taylor had seen up to then. She remembers the huge pressure she felt

"I was quite aware it was a history-making fight because of the attention it was getting in the media beforehand and afterward. I remember being quite nervous on the day because I realized how huge it actually was. The hardest part was the media interest. I was very shy and I hated it. It was a bit much for a girl of 15."

Taylor won the contest on points and went on to dominate women's amateur boxing. It didn't take long before she lifted her first gold medals at the European Championships in Norway and at the Women's World Boxing Championship in China. In the 60 kg weight class, she was unbeatable.

But as she racked up the medals she became involved in a different fight, battling with the International Olympic Committee (IOC) to have women's boxing recognized as an Olympic event.

Taylor had been involved in the lobbying of the IOC to have women's boxing in the Beijing Games of 2008. To show what a great sport it was, she put on exhibition fights in places as far afield as Chicago and St. Petersburg. But the campaign narrowly failed.

She redoubled her efforts for the London Olympics in 2012 with the boxing association using her as the figurehead of their campaign. In 2009, the IOC finally relented and three years later the private and shy Taylor fought her toughest and most public battle yet. At London 2012 she carried the hopes of an entire nation who were willing her to become Ireland's first Olympic gold medalist - in any sport - since 1996. Crowds gathered on the streets of her hometown to watch her bouts on giant screens put up especially for the occasion. There was even a song in the Irish music charts called "Katie Taylor Ireland's Boxing Legend".

And she didn't let them down.

In the final, she came up against the Russian southpaw Sofya Ochigava. That night Taylor was like an artist and the ring was her canvas. Every punch she threw was a beautiful brush stroke. And the final painting was of her wearing a gold medal around her neck. She became the first ever Olympic female lightweight champion. When she went home to Ireland, huge crowds turned up to the airport to show her how much it meant to them.

After the Olympics, Taylor tightened her grip on the lightweight division, winning another European and World Championship in 2014. But as the 2016 Olympic games in Rio-de-Janeiro came around, Katie had a falling out with her dad, who also trained her. That meant she had to get a new coach. But her boxing suffered and she was beaten in the quarter-final in Rio, bringing a sad ending to her Olympic career.

As an amateur boxer she had won everything. Five world titles, six European titles and Olympic gold. And in her final couple of years as an amateur Katie was beginning to fall out of love with boxing. She needed a new challenge to motivate herself. It was time to leave the amateur ranks and go pro.

Taylor turned professional in 2016 and moved to America to train for her first professional bout. This new focus helped her to enjoy boxing again. But it wasn't an easy change and the move to the USA meant making a lot of sacrifices. Her new life was only hard training, reading and going to church. "There are times when it is quite lonely when you are away from your family for so long. I think if you want to achieve greatness in anything there is a price tag for that," she said. And achieve greatness she did.

Taylor made her professional debut on 26 November 2016, scoring a third-round technical knockout (TKO) at the Wembley Arena in London. Taylor's skill and courage meant that she beat every challenger that came her way. In boxing there are four different belts that a boxer can win. By 2019 Katie had three of them, but wanted the fourth to become the undisputed champion. To do this she would need to fight the holder of the fourth belt, Delfine Persoon from Belgium.

Persoon had not lost a fight in 5 years. At that point in time it was the biggest fight in female boxing history. They would face off at the famous Madison Square Garden in New York.

We heard how they battled each other, round after round. Until they were both bruised and battered. Then when it was all over, the referee took Taylors arm and held it high in the air. She had done it. The first undisputed female lightweight champion ever.

She has gone on to defend that title seven times - putting her ahead of famous boxers like George Foreman, Joe Frazier, Floyd Mayweather Jr., and Lennox Lewis in the list of most unified title defenses in a professional career. These challenges saw her win 21 straight bouts. Many of these fights took place on undercards, away from the limelight. But that can't be said of her 2022 title defense. It was the biggest fight of the year for both men and women.

Taylor's opponent was the Puerto Rican Amanda Serrano, herself a world record holder for having won world titles at seven different weights. The fight was the first-ever women's boxing match to top the bill at Madison Square Garden. The ticket revenue of $1.45m was the highest for any event at the Garden since the end of the Covid-19 epidemic. And the worldwide audience of 1.5 million people smashed all previous box-office records for a woman's fight.

The match wasn't just a landmark for women's boxing. It was named Fight of the Year by the WBA, Sports Illustrated and Event of the Year by The Ring magazine. The fight made the fans hold their breath until the final second, with the feeling that either boxer could win at any moment. In the end, the spirit of the two warriors' made them both winners. But it was Taylor that came home with the belts. Her narrow victory over Serrano meant that she was now recognized as the best pound-for-pound female fighter in the world.

Taylor would go on to have more big title fights, losing her belts and getting them back again. All the while showing the heart and skill she had become known for. But outside of the ring Taylor has used her fame to help her community. She became an ambassador for children's hospitals, hospices, and social clubs for disabled people in and around Bray. And she has supported international children's charities like Zest4Kidz in their work worldwide.

Despite all her success, Taylor looks back on the Olympics - first getting women's boxing included, and then winning - as the highlight of her career. Not just because she came home with a gold medal but because she has helped pave the way for generations of female boxers to be able to follow their dreams. Taylor has been a fighter her whole life. Inside and outside the ring. Her determination to not let society control her dreams, shows how powerful a fighting spirit can be.

JIM MORRIS

Picture this. A 35-year-old physics teacher and father of three small kids, coaching a rag-tag high school baseball team in a small Texas town. He makes a deal with his players that if they can somehow win their district championship, he will try out for a Major League Baseball team.

Against all odds, the team turns its season around and makes it to the state playoffs, and the coach - a former Minor League pitcher - winds up throwing 98 mph at the tryout. He is signed by the Tampa Bay Devil Rays, and just a few months later, he joins the big league team on the road in his home state. And in his first game he strikes out the only batter he faces.

That's the story of Jim Morris. It's a great story. An astounding story. A story so good that Walt Disney turned it into a movie "The Rookie". The only rookie with gray hair!

But let's back up a little first.

Morris had been drafted by the New York Yankees straight out of high school but he couldn't go. He wanted to stay at home to help care for his grandfather who was very ill. But the following year the Milwaukee Brewers took him fourth overall in the amateur draft. In his first year he hurt his throwing arm and needed surgery. He was told by the doctor who surgically removed most of his deltoid (shoulder) muscle that he would never pitch again. At the age of 24, Morris had to retire from baseball.

And for most people, that would have been the end of it.

But Morris went back home to Texas and studied to become a teacher. He got a job teaching physical science at Reagan County High School in Big Lake - a football-obsessed town with less than 3,000 people. The whole town could fit into one small corner of Yankee Stadium.

For the 1999 season, Morris became the coach of the school baseball team. But they weren't very good and had won a grand total of three games over the previous three seasons.

He remembers "I had eight kids for the first practice session and had to persuade two others to come. We had batting practice and I liked to pitch from the mound so I could see what they were doing. One day the catcher, Joel, said to me: 'You're hurting my hand, man.' I didn't think I was pitching hard at all. Even when I was in the minors I threw a max of 88mph.

"We lost our first two games. I talked to them about hopes, dreams and goals. I said: 'It's more than baseball. You all need to go out and live life.' The kids were smiling. Joel said: 'What about your dream, coach?' I said 'My dream is to see you succeed in the classroom and on the field.' He said 'We think you still want to play,' so I told him 'I don't have 85% of the muscle in my shoulder and I weigh 260 pounds because your mums keep feeding me tortillas.'

"They saw the joy I had on the mound when I threw.

Joel asked 'Why are you telling us to chase our dreams when you're not even chasing your own? If we win the district championship, you go for the tryout.' So, I did what any parent who wants to see kids succeed would do, and said yes."

That's how the bet came about. And when Reagan County unexpectedly won the district title for the first time in school history, the pupils told Morris he had to keep his side of the deal.

The Tampa Bay Devil Rays were holding a tryout in his hometown, so Morris went along. He thought he would be laughed at, but felt he could manage a few minutes on the mound. At the tryouts, when the scout saw this 'old man', he said "I'll let you throw, but you'll go last."

Morris felt nervous as he threw his first pitch. He could see the scout shaking his radar gun and he thought maybe he was throwing so slow that the speed didn't register on the gun. They made him throw another 60 pitches. Finally Morris stopped because he thought they were making fun of the old fat dude. But the scout came over to show him the screen on the speed gun "You threw your first pitch at 94 mph and it went up to 98mph." Morris' first thought was 'I've been throwing 98 mph at high school kids? – I'm going to get sued."

The scouts didn't care about Morris' age. He was left-handed and throwing balls like they had been shot out of a cannon, exploding in the catcher's mitt. The Devil Rays signed him up quickly, and within a month he was playing Minor League Baseball with the Durham Bulls.

Word got out about the unlikely rookie.

Not long after Morris' first game with the Bulls, sports-agent Steve Canter read a Baseball Weekly article about "the schoolteacher who throws 98 mph". Canter was excited and thought that Morris' journey was so much like a Disney story, maybe it would make a good movie? But to have that fairytale ending, Morris needed to play in the Major Leagues.

When Morris agreed to take Canter on as his agent, he had just been called up to play Triple-A. That's the level just below Major League Baseball. Canter excitedly explained to Morris "tomorrow, you're playing for an organization that's in last place, and you're throwing the baseball really, really well". Morris nodded.

"If you pitch well in Triple-A, the Rays are going to call you up to the big leagues. And if the Rays call you up to the big leagues, I promise you we're going to make a movie about your life, and you're never going to have to worry about being able to take care of your family again."

Morris was stunned. Why would anyone want to make a movie about him? Not many people knew, but Morris was dead broke and hadn't made any money since he left his teaching job. His wife had called him to tell him that their furniture was going to be taken away if they missed payment on any more bills.

Canter told Morris "I hate to tell you this, but you could end up hurting your arm again. But you're going to make your money off the field, and it's going to be because of your amazing story." Morris liked the sound of that.

And sure enough, in mid-September, he got the call to join the big league club, the Tampa Bay Devil Rays.

Morris' wife, Lorri, and their three kids packed into the car and drove nearly four hours to be there for the game. They sang most of the way, giddy with excitement. That night the kids saw their dad for the first time in three months when they peeked into the bullpen before the game.

Morris didn't start the game. But in the bottom of the eighth inning with the Devil Rays trailing, 6-1, Morris was called from the bullpen to face Royce Clayton of the Texas Rangers. The batter had been an All-Star two years earlier.

Jim pulls open the bullpen door and all the smells of baseball – leather, beer, popcorn – hit him like a truck. All the colors of the crowd. It's so loud he can't even hear his family cheering him. Then he smiles to himself when he thinks "I'm here because of a bunch of kids who everyone had counted out."

At the mound, Morris looks the batter in the eye and tips the peak of his black cap. Then throws four fastballs in a row. All clocked at 95 mph or higher. Clayton swings but watches each one fly past his bat. They go so fast they seem to whistle in the air. The commentators laugh "I didn't believe it when I heard about this school teacher, but I do now!".

One batter, one 'out' and one memory to last a lifetime. "Even all these years later," Morris says, "I'm like, 'Did that really happen?"

The next stop on the teams schedule was Anaheim, just outside Los Angeles and not far from the famous Hollywood Hills. When the Devil Rays got there, Morris did an interview with the Los Angeles Times newspaper. The next day, his story was plastered on the sports page under the headline, "Living the Impossible Dream."

All of Hollywood now knew who Jim Morris was, and they all wanted to tell his story. But none of them seemed to be able to tell the story the way Jim thought it should be. "I want a movie that's about a group of kids who are called 'out' before they even started," Morris said. And he wanted it to be about someone who takes a chance on themselves so that they don't wake up every morning thinking 'Why didn't

I try one more time?'"

With a fairytale story like that, it could only be Disney that would do it right. Morris was able to be on the set for a lot of the filming and even made a cameo as an umpire. By that point, his pitching career was over. He played in five games for the Rays in that magical 1999 season and another 16 games in 2000. But after signing with the LA Dodgers for 2001, he had problems with his vision and balance during Spring Training and felt that it was time for him to call it a day.

"I walked into the Dodgers manager's office and said, 'It's time for me to go home,'" Morris recalls. "He hugs me and says, 'If you need anything, call.' Then he sends me through the clubhouse with the clubhouse kid giving me helmets and bats and balls to hand out to the neighborhood kids when I get home. I got home, got my kids and went to the movie set."

The movie was a huge success when it came out in 2002. Disney arranged a dinner in honor of the movie release, with Hall of Famers Willie Mays and Hank Aaron coming along for a look. There was even a screening of the film at the White House for President George W. Bush.

Not long after retiring from baseball, Morris was diagnosed with Parkinson's (a condition that causes problems in the brain). But in spite of the condition, he has managed to jog again and is living an active life, surprising even the most optimistic of his doctors.

Morris is now a little older, a little grayer. His kids are grown and the high school players who inspired him to launch his second pro baseball career are older than he was when he debuted with the Rays.

Morris spent two seasons in Major League Baseball and

in that time no one could explain how a 35-year-old science teacher who ate too many tacos, could throw the ball 10 mph faster than he did as an athletic young man.

Looking back on the journey to his Major League career, Morris still can't believe how it happened. "It was a whole lot shoved into a short period," he says. "It was just boom, boom, boom. And it was all because of a bet with a group of kids. If it hadn't been for those kids, I never would have tried."

Morris showed that it's never too late to follow your dreams and sometimes it's the kids who inspire the adults.

HOW CAN THESE STORIES HELP YOU?

As I researched the stories of these amazing athletes, the same words kept coming up again and again: resilience, perseverance, confidence, teamwork, humility, respect, sportsmanship. What great values to have!

Tony Hawk showed a lot of perseverance in taking ten years to perfect a single trick, before he pulled off the '900'.

Katie Taylor's resilience kept her coming back every time she was told she wasn't allowed to box. She didn't let the rejection break her spirit.

If these stories have shown me anything, it's that it's often the losing and the disappointments that teach us the best lessons.

When we don't win or get the result that we want, we must learn how to deal with the emotions around that. I've often listened to top coaches say that they learn more from losing than winning. A mistake or loss is an opportunity to learn and improve, similar to what old Ben Franklin said about adversity creating opportunities.

I bet that there's been more than one time when you've been faced with something really difficult and you thought "I can't do it."?

Well, sport encourages you to take that phrase and add the word 'yet' at the end. That's maybe the most important thing I've ever learned from playing sports.

And you can take that 'yet' and use it wherever you go and whatever you do, outside of sports.

So the next time you think you're not good enough to make the team, not strong enough to paddle your surfboard out past the waves, not smart enough to pass that exam or creative enough to write that story, just add that 'yet' and go again.

Who knows, maybe someday I'll be writing a story about you!

AFFIRMATIONS

Positive affirmations are phrases that you can use to motivate yourself and to change how you feel about yourself. If you say something over and over, then your brain eventually starts to believe it. You can change the way you think about yourself!

The affirmations opposite are inspired by the athletes in this book. Pick one of the affirmations and repeat it to yourself slowly, ten times. Out loud if you can. Try a different one every day. And if you think of a new one that you like, add it to the list!

- I AM DETERMINED.

- I AM BRAVE.

- I DON'T GIVE UP EASILY.

- I WILL TRY AND TRY AND THEN TRY SOME MORE.

- I AM SUPPORTED.

- I CAN SOLVE PROBLEMS.

- IT'S OKAY TO BE SCARED.

- IT'S OKAY TO BE MYSELF.

- I BELIEVE IN MYSELF.

- MY DIFFERENCES ARE WHAT MAKE ME SPECIAL.

- I ENJOY HELPING OTHER PEOPLE.

- I AM A GOOD TEAMMATE.

- I RESPECT OTHER PEOPLE.

- I CAN BE WHATEVER I WANT TO BE.

- NOBODY CAN STOP ME.

IF YOU DON'T FALL HOW ARE YOU GOING TO KNOW WHAT GETTING UP IS LIKE?

STEPH CURRY

THANK YOU!

I hope that you enjoyed this book. I would really love to hear your thoughts on it.

Many readers don't know how hard reviews are to come by, or how much they help an author.

I would be so grateful if you could take just one minute to write a review on Amazon, even if it's just a sentence or two.

I read all the reviews and it really means a lot. Scanning the QR codes opposite will take you straight to the reviews page. Thank you!!

UK

USA

CANADA

FUN BONUS STUFF

Not all sports stories have to be heroic and serious. Let's finish this book with a smile! Here is some weird and wonderful sports trivia you can use to entertain your friends and family:

FERRET LEGGING

...is a bizarre sport where competitors place live ferrets inside their trousers to see who can endure it the longest. The world record stands at 5 hours and 26 minutes.

TOE WRESTLING

Yes, it's a real sport. Competitors lock toes and attempt to pin each other's foot to the ground. The World Toe Wrestling Championship takes place annually in England.

BED RACING

In Ketchikan, Alaska, teams construct beds with wheels and

race them through the streets as part of the annual Blueberry Festival. The fastest team to push their bed to the finish line wins.

CHEESE ROLLING

In Gloucestershire, England, there's an annual event where participants chase a wheel of cheese down a steep hill. The first person to cross the finish line wins the cheese. It's called the Cooper's Hill Cheese-Rolling and Wake.

QUIDDITCH

Inspired by the fictional sport in the Harry Potter series, real-life Quidditch has become popular. Players run around with brooms between their legs, attempting to score points by throwing balls through hoops.

CRICKET'S LONGEST MATCH

The longest recorded cricket match lasted for 14 days. It took place in 1939 between England and South Africa. The match was called off because the English team had to catch their boat home.

OSTRICH RACING

In some parts of the world, particularly South Africa and the United States, ostrich races are held as entertainment events. Jockeys ride on the backs of these large birds, racing them around a track.

GIGGLE CORNER

TRY THESE JOKES ON YOUR FAMILY
AND SEE IF YOU CAN GET A LAUGH!

WHY DID THE
BICYCLE FALL
OVER DURING THE
RACE?

IT WAS TWO-
TIRED!

WHAT DID THE
BASEBALL GLOVE
SAY TO THE BALL?

"CATCH YA
LATER!"

WHY DID THE
FOOTBALL TEAM
GO TO THE BANK?

TO GET THEIR
QUARTERBACK!

WHY WAS CINDERELLA SO BAD AT SOCCER?

BECAUSE SHE ALWAYS RAN AWAY FROM THE BALL!

WHERE DOES MOST OF A HOCKEY PLAYER'S MONEY COME FROM?

THE TOOTH FAIRY.

IF AT FIRST YOU DON'T SUCCEED, SKYDIVING IS NOT FOR YOU!

WHY ARE BASEBALL GAMES AT NIGHT?

THE BATS SLEEP DURING THE DAY.

WHAT ARE THE RULES FOR ZEBRA BASEBALL?

THREE STRIPES AND YOU'RE OUT.

WHY DO BASKETBALL PLAYERS LIKE COOKIES?

IT'S JUST ANOTHER EXCUSE TO DUNK.

WHICH SPORT IS ALWAYS IN TROUBLE?

BAD-MINTON.

TODAY A MAN KNOCKED ON MY DOOR AND ASKED FOR A SMALL DONATION TOWARDS THE LOCAL SWIMMING POOL. SO I GAVE HIM A GLASS OF WATER.

WHY COULDN'T THE DOG RUN IN THE MARATHON?

BECAUSE HE WASN'T A PART OF THE HUMAN RACE!

WHAT IS CARDBOARD'S FAVORITE SPORT?

BOXING.

I KEPT WONDERING WHY THE BASEBALL WAS GETTING BIGGER.

THEN IT HIT ME.

WHAT'S THE HARDEST THING ABOUT SKATEBOARDING?

CONCRETE.

1 AWESOME SPORTS JOKES AND TRIVIA

2 SPORTS WORD JUMBLE

3 INSPIRING QUOTES

Please have your grown up scan
this QR code with their phone
camera to get the free goodies.